A Taste for Love

ROMANTIC MEALS FOR TWO

Elizabeth M. Harbison AND Mary McGowan

WINGS BOOKS

New York

Acknowledgments

I'd like to gratefully acknowledge the support and help of my husband, John. Thanks for years of great friendship and romance!

Thanks to Annie Jones and Lucinda Denton for E-mailing me so many terrific romantic tips.

Also, thanks to my mother, who helped in a million ways, not the least of which was being on call for kitchen emergencies of all sorts.

Most of all, thanks to my agent, Meg Ruley, for her faith, perseverance, and friendship.

—E. M. H.

To Steve Cohen, the great and only love of my life.

—M^2

Copyright © 1996 by Elizabeth M. Harbison and Mary McGowan
All rights reserved under International and Pan-American Copyright Conventions.
Wings Books and colophon are trademarks of Random House Value Publishing, Inc.

This 1996 edition is published by Wings Books,
a division of Random House Value Publishing, Inc.,
201 East 50th Street, New York, New York 10022,
by arrangement with the authors.

Random House
New York • Toronto • London • Sydney • Auckland
http://www.randomhouse.com/
Book design by Marysarah Quinn
Illustrations by Leslie Wu

Printed and bound in Mexico.

Library of Congress Cataloging-in-Publication Data
Harbison, Elizabeth M.
A taste for love : romantic meals for two / Elizabeth M. Harbison
and Mary McGowan
p.   cm.
ISBN 0-517-14792-0
1. Cookery for two.   I. McGowan, Mary.   II. Title.
641.5'61—dc20   95-38233
CIP

8 7 6 5 4

Contents

Preface

Romance, they say, is about the little things. It's about a feeling, a moment, a memory.

You don't have to be stranded on a tropical island with a case of Dom Pérignon to prove your romantic intentions. Nor do you need to present a diamond ring or a Maserati in order to make someone feel luxuriously indulged.

All you need is desire, time, and a little imagination.

Consider the gift of a great meal. Lovers through the ages have enticed their mates with "a loaf of bread, a jug of wine," oysters, caviar, strawberries and cream, chocolate, champagne, and a host of other personal delicacies. Why? Because they work!

What a delicious sense of well-being, to linger over a satisfying meal with an adored companion, savoring the company, the food, the wine. Add atmosphere with candlelight and soft music, and paradise is no longer lost.

In this book we put together menus that will persuade and excite. We chose each recipe carefully for its flavor, scent, and harmony with the rest of the menu. Thus, each menu is a work of art within itself.

The meals are not always quick—then again, neither is romance—but they are always appealing to the eye, enticing to the nose, and satisfying to the palate.

We hope you enjoy using this book as much as we enjoyed creating it. Bon appétit!

—Elizabeth M. Harbison & Mary McGowan

About the Authors

Elizabeth M. Harbison has made a lifetime study of cooking, both in the U.S. and Europe, and has worked as a private chef in the Washington, D.C. area since 1990. Her kitchen creativity took on new dimensions in 1987 when she met (and married) the grandson of one of the most prominent caterers in Washington's history, and learned some of the trade secrets that pleased the palates of four U.S. presidents. She currently resides in Germantown, Maryland, with her husband, John, and their daughter, Mary Paige.

Mary McGowan learned from her grandmother to appreciate the many facets of well-prepared good food—to enjoy its appearance, to savor its flavors and textures, to linger on a singularly delicious taste. She furthered this experience with formal training at the renowned L'Academie De Cuisine, and has successfully combined both traditional and formal philosophies and techniques to create a signature cooking style. A writer, private chef, and comedic actor, she lives in Alexandria, Virginia, with her husband, Steve Cohen.

Breakfast in Bed

ROMANTIC AWAKENING MENUS

Dominion Sunrise

Eggs Benedict with Virginia Ham
Hollandaise Sauce
Fresh Fruit with Raspberry-Poppy Dressing
Mimosas

This menu takes you back to the days when Williamsburg, Virginia, was the center of the Colonial world. When the settlers colonized the Virginia shoreline, they discovered that their livestock flourished in the favorable climate—especially the pigs! These pigs provided the distinctly flavored bacons and hams for which Virginia has long been famous.

It is a quiet April morning. Early azaleas and dogwoods are in bloom, and lilac scents the whisper of a breeze that toys with the edges of the bedroom curtains. You and your love linger over each other, and over this sumptuous breakfast.

"Folk need a lot of loving in the morning;
the day is all before, with cares beset."

—STRICKLAND GILLIAN, Need of Loving

Eggs Benedict with Virginia Ham

There is nothing more elegant than the delicate flavor of poached eggs wrapped in the velvet of hollandaise sauce! Virginia ham adds an additional facet of smoked spiciness to this recipe.

When poaching the eggs, remember the liquid (which can be water, stock, milk, or even wine—we've used water for this recipe) should be at least 2 inches deep, for the eggs to immerse completely. The liquid should be preheated (simmering) so that the eggs begin cooking as soon as they are added.

2 English muffins, split
1 teaspoon unsalted butter
4 thin slices of Virginia ham (or any ham labeled "country")
4 large eggs
4 splashes white Worcestershire sauce
Freshly chopped parsley

Split the English muffins, toast them, and give them a light coat of butter. Place two halves on each of two warmed plates. Put a slice of Virginia ham on each half.

Pour at least 2 inches of water into a 10-inch skillet and heat on medium-high until simmering. Break the eggs into the simmering water.

Cover the skillet with a tight-fitting lid to contain the heat. Poach for 5 minutes, or until the egg whites are opaque, then remove the eggs and dip them into cold water to retard further cooking.

Don't worry about raggedy egg edges! Trim them off with a paring knife.

Position one egg on each English muffin half, and cover with hollandaise and a splash of Worcestershire. Garnish with a sprinkle of chopped parsley.

Fresh Fruit with Raspberry-Poppy Dressing

The natural sweetness of raspberry vinegar diminishes the need for extra sugar in this ultradelicious fruit salad dressing.

2 tablespoons sugar (or honey)
1/4 teaspoon salt
3 tablespoons raspberry vinegar
1/2 teaspoon Colman's dry English mustard
1/2 teaspoon shallots, minced
1/3 cup peanut oil
1/2 tablespoon poppy seeds

On high speed in a small food processor, combine the sugar, salt, raspberry vinegar, mustard, and shallots. Slowly add the peanut oil until the mixture emulsifies. Pulse in the poppy seeds.

Pour lightly over two plates of fresh fruit. In summer these might include peaches, plums, strawberries, melons, and kiwis. Winter fruit plates might see more of a citrus offering, such as grapefruits and oranges—or apples and even avocados. And of course, seedless red and green grapes are always in season.

The dressing will keep in the refrigerator for about two weeks.

Mimosas

Morning cannot see a more romantic libation than a delicate wine glass filled to the brim with a Mimosa. Its freshly squeezed orange juice is ripe with the promise of a new day, while the bubbly champagne refreshes the lingering memories of the night before.

True Champagne comes from the Champagne region in France and is a blending of black (pinot noir) and white (chardonnay) grapes. Pink champagne gets its color from contact with the black grape skins or by adding red wine.

12 ounces fresh orange juice, pulp and pits removed
4 ounces chilled champagne

Squeeze oranges and strain to remove pits and pulp. Fill two 10-ounce wineglasses with 6 ounces each of the juice, then top each glass off with 2 ounces of champagne.

TIP

❧ Serve a commemoration newspaper with the mimosas—what was the world up to on your love's birthday or your anniversary? Archive editions of the *New York Times*, the *Wall Street Journal*, and the *Los Angeles Times* are available by calling 1-800-221-3221.

Gentle Awakening

Windsor Toast with Maple Rum Syrup
Maple Baked Apples
Link Sausages
Maple-Almond Tea

When spring begins to awaken in New England, the farmers tap their
sugar and rock maple trees, hoping to yield twelve gallons of sap per tree.
Boiled down, forty gallons of the thin sweet sap yields one gallon of pure
New England maple syrup.

For these recipes, use only Grade A maple syrup
made in New England.

"O tender yearning, sweet hoping!
The golden time of first love!
The eye sees the open heaven,
The heart is intoxicated with bliss,
O that the beautiful time of young love
Could remain green forever."

—JOHANN CHRISTOPH FRIEDRICH VON SCHILLER,
"The Song of the Bell"

Windsor Toast with Maple Rum Syrup

Windsor Toast is a perfect bedside breakfast. Or, if you prefer to get up and about, it's also the kind of meal where four hands are welcome in the preparation.

WINDSOR TOAST:
4 slices thickly sliced bread (homemade if possible), slightly stale
2 eggs
1/2 cup evaporated milk
1 teaspoon dark rum (or rum flavoring)
1 teaspoon maple syrup
1/4 teaspoon ground cinnamon
1/4 teaspoon freshly grated nutmeg
1/2 teaspoon vanilla extract
1 teaspoon peanut oil

Place bread in one layer in a shallow baking dish.

Whisk the eggs in bowl until they are a lemon color. Then whisk in the evaporated milk, rum, sugar, cinnamon, nutmeg, and vanilla.

Cover the bread with the egg mixture and refrigerate for 1 hour.

Add the oil to a nonstick griddle and heat until hot. Place the bread on the griddle and cook until crispy brown on one side. Flip the bread and brown the other side.

Serve two pieces of toast for each person, sauced with Maple Rum Syrup and garnished with a strawberry.

MAPLE RUM SYRUP:
1/4 cup maple syrup
3 tablespoons rum (or 1 tablespoon rum extract)
1 tablespoon unsalted butter

Heat the maple syrup, butter, and rum in a saucepan until the mixture bubbles around the edges. Pour it into a small warmed pitcher and serve with the Windsor Toast.

Maple Baked Apples

Today's large variety of apples is available not only in specialty food stores but at your local grocery as well. Try two different apples with this recipe and compare their taste—we suggest you choose from Granny Smith, Empire, or Mountaineer.

2 apples
Light brown sugar
2 tablespoons unsalted butter
Maple syrup
Ground cinnamon
8 whole cloves

Preheat the oven to 300°.

Wash and core the apples, scooping out some of the fruit—DO NOT BREAK THE PEEL ON THE BOTTOM (otherwise all of the filling will fall out).

Stuff each apple three-fourths full with brown sugar, pressing the sugar down firmly with your index finger. Dot the brown sugar with butter. Top off each apple with maple syrup and sprinkle with ground cinnamon. Stick 4 cloves in each apple.

Set the apples in a shallow pan, add ½ cup water to the pan or enough to cover the bottom, and bake for 30 minutes.

Maple-Almond Tea

The unusual blending of maple and almond flavors makes this hot beverage just the cup of tea to round out this menu.

2 tea bags
3 cups water
2 tablespoons maple sugar
1 teaspoon almond extract
½ teaspoon vanilla extract

Steep the tea bags in 1 cup boiling water for 10 minutes; remove tea bags. In a small saucepan, boil the remaining 2 cups of water and the maple syrup for 5 minutes, then add the almond and vanilla flavorings. Combine the liquids and bring to a boil.

Tips

❦ Enjoy this meal after an early morning hot-air balloon ride. Check your yellow pages to see who offers this service in your area.

❦ *Sunday Morning Coffee*, Volumes I and II, provides soothing wake-up music—classical and contemporary. It features a variety of artists, including Jackson Berkey, Arnie Roth, and Chip Davis.

Cozumel Dawn

Frittata Ranchera
Fresh Fruit Medley
Sautéed Provolone Cheese
Mexican Café

✷

The aqua blue water of the Cozumel tide greets the white sandy shore like a long-lost lover. Fingers of warm salty water caress each grain of sand, lingering until, reluctantly, it is time to leave. Crystalline skies watch overhead, sending bright white puffs of clouds scudding across to provide a temporary respite of shadow.

"If all the world and love were young
And truth in every shepherd's tongue,
These pretty pleasures might me move
To live with thee and be thy love."

—SIR WALTER RALEIGH,
"The Nymph's Reply to the Shepherd"

Frittata Ranchera

In America they are known as hearty pancake-style omelettes; in Provence they go by *crespeus*; by *tortillas* in Spain; and by *frittatas* in Mexico and Italy. Regardless of the language, it translates to an egg dish that contains more flavoring than egg.

This frittata is too bulky to roll or fold, so serve it flat and cut into decorative wedges.

1 tablespoon unsalted butter
1 tablespoon peanut oil
2¹/₂ medium russet potatoes, diced (¹/₂-inch)
1¹/₂ tablespoon flour
¹/₂ teaspoon sweet paprika
¹/₄ teaspoon minced garlic
¹/₂ teaspoon fresh basil, minced
¹/₂ teaspoon fresh oregano, minced
¹/₂ teaspoon fresh parsley, minced
4 eggs, beaten
¹/₈ cup freshly grated Parmesan cheese
2 dashes Tabasco
Salt and freshly ground black pepper to taste
Fresh parsley sprigs

In a plastic bag, mix the potatoes, flour, paprika, garlic, basil, oregano, and parsley.

In a small sauté pan, melt the butter and oil over medium heat and add the potato/flour/spice mixture. Cook until potatoes are fork-tender, about 10 minutes. Set this aside.

Whisk eggs, Parmesan cheese, and Tabasco in a small bowl, seasoning the mixture with salt and pepper.

Pour the egg mixture over the potatoes. Pierce holes in mixture and lift edges with spatula to allow uncooked eggs to flow underneath. DO NOT STIR. Reduce the heat to low, cover the sauté pan, and continue cooking until the frittata is set, about 10 minutes.

Invert on a plate and cut into wedges. Garnish with fresh parsley.

Fresh Fruit Medley

Raspberries are so fragrant and flavorful that even a few will make themselves known in a large fruit salad. Although we are most familiar with red or black raspberries, they can also be yellow, purple, or white.

Beware when buying strawberries—oftentimes the bigger the berry, the blander it is.

Kiwi is a fruit native to New Zealand and indeed named after the kiwi bird. The kiwi's tiny black seeds are edible, giving the fruit a rather crunchy texture.

1/4 cup raspberries (fresh or frozen)
1 teaspoon fresh lime juice
1/2 tablespoon honey
1/2 pint strawberries, hulled and halved
2 kiwis, peeled and sliced
4 spearmint leaves

In a blender or small food processor, puree the raspberries, then strain the puree to remove the seeds. Whisk in the lime juice and honey.

In a small bowl, mix together the kiwis and strawberries and split the mixture into two servings.

Drizzle raspberry sauce lightly over each serving, adding mint leaves for garnish.

Sautéed Provolone Cheese

This imparts delicious, smoky strips that are an excellent alternative to bacon or sausage.

Ask your deli to cut slightly thicker slices of provolone—perhaps 4 millimeters, give or take. Shaved provolone will also work, so don't sweat too much over how thick it is when you begin.

1/4 pound provolone cheese
Vegetable cooking spray

Spray cooking spray on a nonstick frying pan and heat on medium-high flame.

Slice the provolone into finger-size lengths. Fry the cheese on one side until bubbly. Flip it with a spatula and sauté for another 45 seconds. Serve and enjoy!

TIPS

❧ Plant a tree to celebrate your love.

❧ Remember Sergio Mendes? He's back with a tremendously exciting offering called *Brasileiro*. It's a samba-reggae, samba-funk kind of excitement.

By the Fire

ROMANTIC MEALS TO ENJOY BY A ROARING FIRE

The New Traditional

Lentil Soup
Butter Biscuits
City Shepherd's Pie
Apples with Melted Brie
Black and Tan

This is definitely an indoor picnic meal, perfect for a blustery winter's night. Because it is full of hearty flavors, we recommend serving this dinner with strong ale. However, if you're a teetotaler, a nonalcoholic malt brew works equally well.

If you want to serve a wine with dessert, choose a vintage port to blend nicely with the apples.

"But I, fulfilled of my heart's desire
Shedding my song upon height, upon hollow
From tawny body and sweet small mouth,
Feed the heart of the night with fire."

—A. T. SWINBURNE, "Itylus"

Lentil Soup

This is a traditional French country soup that has gained favor all over the world, in part because delicious, smoky-flavored lentils are so nutritious and low in fat.

1 small onion, peeled and chopped
1 tablespoon butter, unsalted
1 clove garlic, peeled and minced
1/2 cup dry lentils, rinsed
2 cups vegetable stock
1 tablespoon lemon juice
Salt and freshly ground black pepper to taste
4 teaspoons chopped fresh parsley

Melt the butter in a medium saucepan over low heat and sauté the onion for 10 minutes. Add to this the garlic, lentils, and vegetable stock. Increase the heat, bringing the liquid to a boil, and boil for 2 minutes.

Reduce the heat to low and simmer the soup gently for 15 to 20 minutes, or until the lentils are soft.

Puree mixture in a blender, food processor, or with an immersion blender. Return to the saucepan and add the lemon juice, salt, and pepper.

Stir well, garnish with parsley, and serve.

Butter Biscuits

Homemade butter biscuits are better by far than store bought.

These hot buttery biscuits are perfect for sopping up any leftover City Shepherd's Pie gravy.

You may add 1/2 cup of grated sharp Cheddar to the batter to make cheese biscuits.

1 cup bread flour, sifted
2 teaspoons baking powder
1/4 teaspoon salt
1 tablespoon unsalted butter, softened
1/3 cup buttermilk (or plain milk with 1 teaspoon vinegar added—let this combination sit for a few minutes)
Melted butter

Preheat the oven to 450°.

Sift the flour, baking soda, and salt into a large mixing bowl. Add the softened butter and stir well. Add milk gradually, until a soft butterlike dough is formed.

Roll or press dough to 1/2-inch thick on slightly floured board. Cut with floured biscuit cutter or the rim of a glass.

Brush melted butter on the top of each biscuit, then place the biscuits on an ungreased baking sheet and bake for 12 to 15 minutes.

City Shepherd's Pie

We used to so enjoy the shepherd's pie served to us by a British friend, until we realized that he cooks with a traditional English flair that limits spicing! Ours is a more flavorful version, which can be made with turkey if you are watching calories, and one that freezes well.

1/2 pound ground round (or turkey)
1 medium onion, chopped
1 clove garlic, minced
1/2 can diced tomatoes
1/2 can sliced water chestnuts, chopped
1 cup hot water
1 package brown gravy mix
1/2 cup frozen peas and carrots, thawed
1 teaspoon finely chopped fresh basil
1 teaspoon finely chopped fresh oregano
1 teaspoon finely chopped fresh parsley
2 small bay leaves
1 teaspoon Worcestershire sauce
2 dashes Tabasco
Paprika
2 cups mashed potatoes (instant are fine)

Preheat the oven to 350°.

In a small nonstick sauté pan over medium-high heat, brown the ground round, drain it, and set it aside.

In the same pan, sauté the onions over low heat until soft, about 5 minutes. Add the ground round to the onions.

Thoroughly mix powdered gravy and hot water in a measuring cup.

To onion and ground round, add the gravy mixture, garlic, tomatoes, water chestnuts, and peas and carrots. Stir over medium heat until gravy simmers.

Stir in basil, oregano, parsley, bay leaves, Worcestershire sauce, and Tabasco. Cover, turn the heat to low, and simmer for 15 minutes.

Cook mashed potatoes according to package directions.

Pour ground round mixture into 2-quart baking dish. Top it with the mashed potatoes. Sprinkle with paprika.

Bake, uncovered, for 35 minutes.

Black and Tan

This is a popular drink in the pubs of England and is a nice alternative for those who can't quite take the heaviness of a stout.

All you do is combine half a mug of stout (such as Guinness or Whatney's Cream Stout) and half a mug of your favorite lager (Samuel Adams is terrific).

That's it!

Winter Passion

Peasant Bread
Garlic and Vegetable Soup over Bread
Baked Butternut Cream
Caramel Fondue
Apple Knockers

This is a delightful meal to warm the soul. This soup is always a hit, even with those who think they don't like vegetable soups. If you have French onion soup bowls, serve the soup in those with the lids on for a lovely presentation.

We recommend serving a light chianti with dinner (Carlo Rossi—yes, an INEXPENSIVE JUG WINE—is perfect both for drinking and for the soup) and saving the apple knockers for afterward with the fondue.

If you have a red-and-white checkered tablecloth, spread it out on the floor for an indoor picnic.

"But true love is a durable fire,
In the mind ever burning."

—SIR WALTER RALEIGH, "The Phoenix Nest"

Peasant Bread

This makes one 1-pound loaf of bread, so you will have leftovers . . . try using it for the Windsor Toast in the Gentle Awakening menu.

1 package dry yeast
2 cups flour
1 teaspoon sugar
1 teaspoon salt
$^1/_4$ teaspoon baking soda
$^3/_4$ cup whole milk
3 tablespoons water
1 tablespoon cornmeal

Preheat the oven to 400°.

Combine the yeast, sugar, salt, baking soda, and 1 cup of the flour in a large bowl. Stir briefly with a wooden spoon to distribute the ingredients. Set the bowl aside.

Heat the liquids in a small saucepan over a medium flame. When they reach a simmer add them to the dry mixture and mix well. Gradually stir in the rest of the flour to make a stiff batter. Knead for 5 minutes.

Grease an 8 by 4-inch loaf pan. Put the bread batter into it and sprinkle the top of the loaf lightly with cornmeal.

Cover the loaf with a dish towel and let it rise in a warm place for 45 minutes.

Bake for 25 minutes, until top is golden brown.

Garlic and Vegetable Soup over Bread

This soup is so simple, yet so elegant. Yes, this recipe calls for lots of garlic, but it can be eliminated entirely for those who are not fond of it.

The chicken broth can be replaced by either vegetable or beef broth, depending on your tastes.

Carlo Rossi Light Chianti makes an excellent broth, although you can use whatever wine you prefer, red or white. But never, ever use a wine that you wouldn't drink (such as store-bought "cooking wine" or red wine that is beginning to turn to vinegar).

1 cup chicken broth
1 cup dry red wine
1 cup crushed tomatoes
1 cup frozen mixed vegetables, thawed
1 medium yellow onion, diced
10 cloves garlic, peeled and minced
2 tablespoons olive oil
1 stalk celery, with leaves
Salt and freshly ground black pepper to taste
2 leaves fresh basil

Heat the olive oil in small sauté pan over medium-high flame until hot. Sauté the onion and 5 cloves of the garlic for 10 minutes. Remove the mixture from the heat and set aside.

In a small saucepan, heat the chicken broth, wine, and crushed tomatoes over medium heat. Add the onion and garlic mixture, then add the mixed vegetables. Cover and simmer for 30 minutes.

Meanwhile, take the remaining 5 cloves of garlic and process them in the blender or food processor along with the celery stalk. Set it aside.

Season the soup with salt and pepper to taste. Simmer 5 minutes more, then stir in the garlic and celery mixture.

Tear slices of Peasant Bread into small pieces and pour soup over it. Garnish with basil and serve immediately.

TIPS

❧ Have a star named in honor of your love by calling the International Star Registry at 1-800-282-3333. (This requires at least six weeks' notice.)

❧ John Tesh's *Sax by the Fire* is a sexy, mellow collection of love songs—perfect for sitting by the fire with your love.

Baked Butternut Cream

This warming dish is a traditional New England favorite. If you are concerned about fat, use half-and-half instead of heavy cream.

1 small butternut squash (about 1 pound)
1/2 teaspoon salt
1/2 teaspoon cinnamon, ground
1/4 cup plus 2 tablespoons heavy cream

Preheat the oven to 350°.

Peel and grate the squash and place into a small bowl.

Gently stir the salt into grated squash; transfer the mixture to an ungreased casserole dish.

Dust the squash with cinnamon and pour the cream over the whole mixture.

Bake, covered, for 45 minutes. Remove the cover and bake another 10 to 15 minutes, until lightly brown.

Caramel Fondue

This is a variation on the chocolate fondue dessert, and the brandy adds a sophisticated twist.

6 ounces evaporated milk
12 caramels
1 tablespoon plus 1 teaspoon brandy
1/2 teaspoon vanilla extract
Bite-size pieces of any or all: apples, bananas, peaches, pears

Heat the evaporated milk and caramels in small skillet over low flame. Stir until the caramels have melted thoroughly into the milk.

Increase the heat to medium and simmer 5 minutes, or until mixture thickens. Remove the pan from the heat and add the brandy and vanilla.

Place the mixture in fondue pot.

Put the fruit in a bowl in the center of the table, next to the melted caramel fondue, and provide fondue sticks for dipping.

Apple Knockers

This recipe (which makes two large mugs' worth) can be doubled, tripled, and so on, and makes a fantastic warmer for Thanksgiving, Christmas, New Year's, Valentine's Day, or any other time you want a spicy warm concoction.

If you don't have cheesecloth, you can put the spices directly into the liquids and pour your drinks through a fine strainer or a coffee filter.

1 cinnamon stick
1/2 teaspoon whole cloves
1 pinch nutmeg
1 1/2 cups apple cider
1/4 cup sugar
1/2 cup orange juice
2 tablespoons fresh lemon juice
1/4 cup brandy

Tie the cinnamon stick, cloves, and nutmeg in a cheesecloth bag.

In a small saucepan, bring apple cider to a simmer over medium-high heat; add the spice bag and simmer for 15 minutes.

Stir in the sugar. Add the orange and lemon juices. Taste for sweetness and add more sugar if you like.

Add brandy and heat thoroughly just before serving.

Hungry Lovers' Dinner

Kentucky Beer Cheese
Oven-Baked Beef Stew
Warm Dinner Rolls
Sweet Baked Apples
Spiced Winter Beer

This is the perfect meal to eat when coming in from the cold,
perhaps after a day of cross-country skiing or after a long,
romantic walk through snowy woods.

Spiced winter beers are becoming more and more available, thanks to the
efforts of microbreweries, nearly all of which have their own brand of
winter beer. Some of our favorites include Samuel Adams (who makes a
variety of winter beers) and Pete's Wicked Winter Ale.

If you prefer to serve wine instead of beer, go for a sturdy red, such as
pinot noir, Hermitage, Pomerol, or St. Emilion.

"That all-softening, overpowering knell,
The tocsin of the soul—the dinner bell!"

—LORD BYRON, "Don Juan"

Kentucky Beer Cheese

This cheese is addictive—which is, actually, why it was invented. The story is that a Kentucky pub came up with this spicy spread to make patrons thirsty so they'd keep buying beer.

These days it's a Kentucky tradition, and various "homemade" brands of it can be found in grocery stores across the Blue Grass State.

Keep in mind that the beer you use maintains much of its flavor in this spread, so if you use a strong imported beer, the spread will have a particularly hearty flavor.

1/2 pound sharp cheddar cheese, grated
2 cloves garlic, minced
1/2 cup beer
1 pinch salt
1 pinch cayenne pepper
1/2 teaspoon Worcestershire sauce
1 dash Tabasco

Whip all the ingredients together in a blender or food processor, then transfer the mixture to a pretty bowl for serving.

Chill and serve with crackers or melba rounds.

Oven-Baked Beef Stew

The onion soup mix is the "secret ingredient" in this easy but impressive beef stew. We prefer the Chef Boyardee beef gravy, although any will do.

This is a forgiving recipe and if you don't use the best cut of meat, the dish will still be delicious.

Also, a large oven cooking bag (found near the aluminum foil in the grocery store) works just as well as a Dutch oven and makes cleanup a lot easier. If you use a cooking bag, remember to poke a few holes in the top to allow air to circulate—so the bag doesn't blow up!

1/2 pound lean beef for stew
1 potato, peeled and quartered
2 carrots, scrubbed and sliced
1 small onion, peeled and chopped
2 small stalks celery, scrubbed and chopped
1 envelope dry onion soup mix
Salt and freshly ground black pepper to taste
1 cup tomato sauce
1/2 cup prepared beef gravy
1/3 cup water
2 tablespoons gravy or sifted flour
1/2 cup water

Preheat the oven to 275°.

Combine the beef and vegetables in a heavy pot or Dutch oven. Sprinkle with onion soup mix and season with the salt and pepper. Pour on the tomato sauce, gravy, and $1/3$ cup water; stir to mix.

Cover and bake for 4 hours.

Pour the stew into a large saucepan and set on medium heat.

Combine the flour and $1/2$ cup water in a cup and blend until smooth. Add to the stew and cook until the liquid thickens.

Serve.

Sweet Baked Apples

Honey-roasted peanuts or almonds are especially nice in this autumn dessert.

2 Granny Smith apples
2 tablespoons granola or Grape Nuts cereal
2 tablespoons finely minced peanuts and/or
   almonds
$1/4$ teaspoon cinnamon
1 tablespoon honey

Preheat oven to 375°.

Core apples and combine the remaining ingredients to fill each one.

Place apples in a shallow baking dish with $1/2$ cup of water or enough to cover the bottom of the dish to keep them from drying out. Bake for 40 minutes. Serve warm or cool.

TIPS

❧ Core apples and use them as candleholders. Red apples and gold candles are a lovely combination.

❧ Another dessert idea: break thick chocolate bars into chunks and place the chunks into wine goblets with a slice of strawberry for garnish on the side of the glass.

❧ Beethoven's sonatas make nice romantic background music. Make sure your recording includes the famous "Moonlight Sonata."

❧ Line a bowl with aluminum foil and put cool-burning white Christmas lights in, then cover with clear marbles or other nonflammable reflectors. This makes a gorgeous centerpiece and produces a small amount of flattering light.

❧ Windham Hill's first "Winter Solstice" sampler album is perfect with this meal by the fire.

Table for Two

ROMANTIC RESTAURANT MENUS

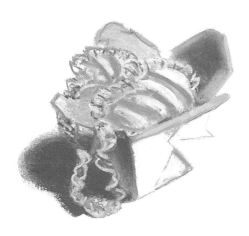

Old Town Fantasy

Baked Onion and Garlic Soup
121 Prince Street Pork Tenderloin with Calvados Sauce
Baron Cameron Glazed Carrots
Sour Cream Rolls
Pears and Stilton

Let your imagination turn back in time. A frosty wind curls through the tavern's ill-fitting windows, but you and your love are safe by the fire, feasting on the innkeeper's sumptuous fare and gazing into each other's eyes.

"Oh you whom I often and silently come where you are that I may be with you,
As I walk by your side or sit near, or remain in the same room with you,
Little you know the subtle electric fire that for your sake is playing within me."

—WALT WHITMAN,
"Oh You Whom I Often and Silently Come"

Baked Onion and Garlic Soup

This rich and creamy soup offers a pleasant surprise in that it is thickened with potato, but tastes like it's thickened with cream!

1 large onion, unpeeled
4 garlic cloves, unpeeled
3 cups vegetable broth, canned or homemade
1 teaspoon Beau Monde seasoning
$^3/_4$ teaspoon dried thyme
$^1/_3$ cup peeled and finely diced russet potato
3 tablespoons croutons
2 sprigs fresh thyme

Preheat the oven to 325°.

Completely cover the onion and garlic cloves in separate aluminum foil envelopes. Place them on a baking sheet in oven and roast until they're tender—about 30 minutes for the garlic, an hour for the onion. Remove them from the oven and let them cool. Squish the garlic from its skin and mash; peel the onion and slice.

In a small saucepan over medium-high heat, bring the vegetable broth to a boil. Add the onions and garlic and bring it to a boil again. Add the Beau Monde and thyme. Reduce the heat to low and simmer for 15 minutes. Add the diced potato and simmer until tender, about 15 minutes. Let the mixture cool, and puree it in a blender, food processor, or with an immersion blender.

Return the soup to the saucepan and bring it to a simmer over medium-high heat. Thin with additional broth if desired.

Ladle into soup bowls and garnish with fresh thyme sprigs and croutons.

121 Prince Street Pork Tenderloin with Calvados Sauce

Good friend Ruth Padgett provided this recipe from her collection of catering "Best Bets." In addition to being known far and wide for her cooking and hostessing acumen, she also has a reputation for being a wise purveyor of real estate. When renovating her 1820s townhouse, she had her master bathroom constructed around the existing marble fireplace. A few bubbles, a little candlelight, a little wine, and voilá—romance!

PORK TENDERLOIN:
1 pound pork tenderloin
2 tablespoons unsalted butter
1 tablespoon flour
1/2 tablespoon Colman's dry English mustard
1 tablespoon cracked peppercorns
1/2 tablespoon mustard seeds
1/2 tablespoon dark brown sugar
1 teaspoon dried thyme

Preheat the oven to 475°.

In a small bowl, mix butter, flour, mustard, peppercorns, mustard seeds, brown sugar, and thyme until pasty. Dry the tenderloin with a paper towel, then completely coat with the coating mixture.

Place the tenderloin in a small roasting pan and cook at 475° for 15 minutes. Reduce oven heat to 325° and roast for 40 more minutes. Let it stand for 5 minutes.

CALVADOS SAUCE:
3/4 cup apple cider (reduced to 1/3 cup)
1 tablespoon unsalted butter
1 tablespoon flour
1/3 cup chicken stock
1/2 tablespoon balsamic vinegar
1/2 tablespoon country-style Dijon mustard
1 1/2 tablespoons Calvados

In a small pan over high heat, bring 3/4 cup apple cider to a boil, and boil down to 1/3 cup. Set it aside. In a small sauté pan over medium-high heat, melt the butter and add the flour.

Whisk for 30 seconds; add the chicken stock and whisk until smooth. Stir in the remaining ingredients, one at a time.

Slice tenderloin on the diagonal and drizzle liberally with Calvados Sauce.

Baron Cameron Carrots

Although this recipe calls for sliced carrots, you may choose to use bagged baby carrots instead. They are young and sweet, and you never run the risk of having to keep your eyes open for a woody (and tasteless) core.

1³/₄ cups carrots, cooked and sliced
3 cups water
1 teaspoon unsalted butter
¹/₈ cup light brown sugar
¹/₈ cup frozen orange juice concentrate, thawed

Slice carrots into thin rounds. In a small saucepan over medium-high heat, bring the water to a boil, then add the carrots. Cook for 15 minutes or until fork-tender. Set them aside.

In a small sauté pan over medium heat, melt the butter and brown sugar together. Add the orange juice concentrate and whisk until blended. Bring to a simmer, stirring frequently for 4 minutes or until thickened. Add the carrots and cook, stirring frequently, until the carrots are heated through.

Sour Cream Rolls

The 121 Prince Street Pork is terrific as a cold sandwich, sliced and sauced on these Sour Cream Rolls, which—by the way, work just as well if you substitute light sour cream.

1 package dry yeast
1 tablespoon sugar
1 tablespoon plus 1 teaspoon warm water
³/₄ cup sour cream
1 teaspoon salt
1 pinch baking soda
1¹/₂ to 2 cups flour

Preheat the oven to 375°.

Combine the yeast, sugar, and warm water in a cup and set aside.

Mix the sour cream, salt, and baking soda in a medium bowl. Stir in 1 cup of the flour, as well as the yeast/sugar/water mixture, and mix thoroughly.

When you have a well-combined sticky dough, add the remaining flour bit by bit until the dough is slightly sticky to the touch.

Put the dough in a greased bowl, cover, and let it rise in a warm, undrafty place for an hour—it will double in bulk.

Punch the dough down, turn it onto a floured board, and knead it for a minute. Let it stand for 5 minutes.

Grease an 8 by 8-inch baking dish.

Divide the dough into 10 even pieces and space them evenly in the baking dish. Cover with a cloth and put it back in that undrafty place to rise (45 minutes to 1 hour).

Bake the rolls for 25 to 30 minutes, or until they're golden brown on top.

TIPS

❦ If you are serving vintage port, use tulip-shaped glasses designed expressly for port or madeira.

❦ Thinking about presenting a ring? Bake it into one of the rolls—make sure you tear the rolls before eating, though!

❦ *Symphonic Music of the Rolling Stones*— lush and fully orchestrated, this is a new and unusual way to experience Mick and the Boys.

Pears and Stilton

This is such an uncomplicated dessert, yet so classically elegant and rich.

Comb your local grocery store for a variety of pears; the spicy-sweet Comice with its fine-grained, juicy flesh, and the deliciously musky Bartlett are considered best for eating raw. The Anjou and smaller Bosc have firmer flesh and are ideal for baking.

If you really want a taste treat, order Royal Riviera pears from Harry and David (the celebrated mail-order fruit company). Available in the fall and winter, these pears are rich and sweet and oh-so-juicy! The toll-free number is 1-800-547-3033.

Serve the pears alongside slices of the "king of cheese"—one of England's proudest moments, the firm, slightly crumbly Stilton. Milder than France's Roquefort or Italy's Gorgonzola, this blue cheese's tangy flavor complements the sweetness of the pears.

Sip port as you nibble. Port, a fortified wine, is named after the city Oporto in Portugal. A ruby port, with its mature resonance and deep clarity, is a sublime experience. But even an immature port can be tamed by the presence of the cheese.

Savor this dessert and enjoy your conversation and company.

New York Masquerade

Waldorf Salad
Wall Street Tenderloin with Horseradish Chive Sauce
Creamed Spinach
Times Square Potatoes
Broadway Cappuccino Custard
Merlot or Shiraz

It is just before dawn. The sirens and horns that screamed through the night have faded into the distance. You walk hand in hand, exhausted by the hour, exhilarated by the romance. A carriage clops by and you hitch a ride. And as the city comes slowly to life, you realize that your life will not be complete without the person you hold so closely in your arms.

"Say not 'Good Night'; but in some brighter clime
Bid me 'Good Morning.'"

—ANNA LETITIA BARBAULD, "Ode to Life"

Wall Street Tenderloin with Horseradish Chive Sauce

So simple and yet so elegant. Be sure to purchase "prime" rather than "choice" tenderloin because the "prime" inspection label ensures that you have the very best.

The delicate taste of the tenderloin invites a red wine, but something lighter than a Cabernet Sauvignon—perhaps a California merlot or an Australian Shiraz.

WALL STREET TENDERLOIN:
1 pound beef tenderloin, center cut
1 tablespoon garlic powder
1 tablespoon black pepper
1 tablespoon paprika

Preheat the oven to 325°.
Rinse the tenderloin and pat it dry with a paper towel.
Mix the spices together and rub over the tenderloin. Let stand 15 minutes, then repeat the rub.
Place the tenderloin on a broiling pan and roast it for 25 minutes. Remove from the oven and let stand for 5 minutes.
With a sharp knife, cut the tenderloin into generous slices and serve.

HORSERADISH CHIVE SAUCE:
1/8 cup salad dressing (such as Miracle Whip)
1/8 cup sour cream
1 tablespoon prepared horseradish
1 teaspoon chives, freshly chopped
1 teaspoon capers, small

In a small food processor, blend together the salad dressing, sour cream, and horseradish until the mixture is creamy. Then pulse in chives and capers.
Serve as an accompaniment to the tenderloin.

Waldorf Salad

The year is 1893, opening night at William Waldorf Astor's new hotel, the Waldorf-Astoria. Chef Noillard enthusiastically unveils a salad that is still popular more than a century later.

1 large red Delicious apple, cut into 1/2-inch pieces
1/2 cup celery, cut into 1/2-inch pieces
1/8 cup chopped walnuts
1/8 cup mayonnaise

Combine the apple, celery, and nuts in small bowl. Dress mixture with the mayonnaise and serve.

Creamed Spinach

When coauthor Mary McGowan tasted Steve Cohen's recipe for creamed spinach, she knew she was in love forever.

1 package frozen spinach
1 cup water
2 tablespoons unsalted butter
2 tablespoons flour
1 tablespoon fresh lemon juice
1/2 cup whole milk
2 tablespoons sugar
1/2 teaspoon garlic powder
1/2 teaspoon freshly ground black pepper
Nutmeg

Place the frozen spinach and water in a small saucepan and bring to a simmer over medium-high heat. Cook until no ice is left in the mixture. Remove it from the heat, strain, and reserve 1 cup of "spinach juice."

In a small sauté pan, whisk the butter until melted. Whisk in the flour and cook for 30 seconds. Whisk in spinach juice a little at a time, add the lemon juice, and whisk in the milk. When the mixture is thick and creamy, whisk in the sugar, garlic powder, and pepper.

Add spinach to the roux and mix well. Sprinkle individual servings with nutmeg.

This recipe reheats well.

Times Square Potatoes

These potatoes are delicious, uncomplicated, and always a fine accompaniment to roast meats.

1 1/2 cups potato balls
1/2 teaspoon salt
5 cups water
1 teaspoon unsalted butter
1 tablespoon peanut oil
1/2 teaspoon paprika
Salt and ground white pepper to taste
Parsley

Scoop potato balls from large potatoes with a small melon-baller.

Place potato balls in cold salted water in a medium saucepan and bring to a boil over medium-high heat. Reduce the heat to medium, simmer uncovered for 5 minutes, then drain.

Heat the butter and oil in small sauté pan over medium heat. Add the potato balls and sauté for 15 minutes or until crispy brown. Add the paprika, salt, and pepper.

Garnish with parsley and serve.

Broadway Cappuccino Custard

Is there anything more delicious than a cool, creamy custard! Gentle baking in a water bath is the key to success.

¹/₂ cup half-and-half
¹/₈ cup lightly ground coffee beans
¹/₈ cup sugar
1 pinch cinnamon
1 pinch nutmeg
¹/₄ cup chilled heavy cream
1 egg yolk
1 egg
¹/₂ ounce milk-chocolate shavings

Preheat the oven to 350°.

Combine the half-and-half, coffee beans, sugar, cinnamon, and nutmeg in a small saucepan and whisk over medium-high heat until the sugar dissolves. Bring the mixture to a simmer. Remove from the heat and let it stand in the pot for 20 minutes.

Strain the mixture into a small bowl. Add the heavy cream, egg, and egg yolk. Whisk until smoothly blended.

Divide the mixture into two custard cups or ramekins and place in a glass baking pan. Add water in the pan to come up halfway on custard cups, and cover the baking pan with aluminum foil.

Bake for 30 minutes, or until the custard is set in the center. Remove the cups from the baking dish and place in the refrigerator overnight.

Sprinkle the tops with chocolate shavings before serving.

TIPS

❦ Give your love a silver-framed picture of the two of you—wrap it in a box from Tiffany, and use it as the base of your table's centerpiece.

❦ *Aspects of Andrew Lloyd Webber,* performed by the BBC Concert Orchestra, highlights the composer's greatest shows on Broadway!

Hollywood Nights

Nutty Wild Nights Salad
Studio Chicken in Phyllo
Oscar's Potatoes
Emmy's Elegant Vegetable Medley
Chocolate Mousse
Sauvignon Blanc

The glamour, the excitement, and the lure of Hollywood brought you from
a small town in a small state to the sun of California to seek your fortune.
But the turn of fortune was unexpected. For sitting across from you
at your table, with a hand lightly touching yours, is the face you admired
on the big screen. The face that everyone knows. The face that is
now part of your life.

The wine you sip with this meal is white and dry—it tickles your tongues
in anticipation—a California sauvignon blanc.

*"If you but knew
How all my days seem filled with dreams of you."*

—UNKNOWN, "If You But Knew"

Nutty Wild Nights Salad

This is a flavorful salad, made interesting by the smoky addition of toasted hazelnut.

1/4 cup wild rice
1 cup beef stock
1 tablespoon red wine vinegar
1/2 tablespoon soy sauce
1/2 teaspoon sugar
1/8 cup peanut oil
1 teaspoon sesame oil
1/2 cup peas
1 stalk celery, sliced thinly on diagonal
2 scallions, sliced thinly
1/8 cup hazelnut pieces, toasted
2 lettuce leaves

Place rice in a small saucepan. Cover the rice with cold water to 1 inch above rice and heat to boiling over a medium high flame. Drain the water from the rice, add the stock, and simmer, covered, until the liquid is absorbed.

Combine the vinegar, soy sauce, sugar, peanut oil, and sesame oil in a small bowl. Whisk until the sugar dissolves.

Toss rice with dressing, then cool.

In a small bowl, combine the rice and dressing mixture with the peas, celery, scallions, and hazelnuts. Toss well and refrigerate.

Serve on a bed of lettuce leaves.

Oscar's Potatoes

Sure, you could bake or mash a potato to go with this, but why be ordinary? Forget the diet for the night. Love, as we know, burns calories . . .

1 large russet potato, peeled, cooked, and mashed
2 slices bacon, fried crisp and crumbled
2 tablespoons unsalted butter, melted
1 tablespoon chopped finely fresh chives
1 pinch salt
Flour
1 small egg, beaten
1/4 cup crushed almonds
Peanut oil

In a small bowl, combine the mashed potatoes, bacon, butter, chives, and salt. Chill this mixture in the refrigerator for at least 2 hours. Shape the mixture into 1-inch balls.

Roll the balls in the flour, then dip them in the beaten egg. Roll in the crushed almonds.

Heat 2 inches of peanut oil so it pops if you drip water in. Drop the potato balls into the hot oil and fry until golden brown.

Drain and serve immediately. These are especially good with a dip of blue cheese dressing.

Studio Chicken in Phyllo

Purchase phyllo dough in the frozen food section of your grocery store. Be sure to keep it moist by covering it with a damp towel as you are working with it or it will dry and crumble in your hands.

1 chicken breast, boneless, skinless and cut into
    $1/2$-inch pieces
1 tablespoon flour
1 teaspoon peanut oil
1 teaspoon seasoned salt
$1/8$ cup country Dijon mustard
1 tablespoon finely chopped fresh tarragon
$1/3$ cup heavy cream
$1/4$ cup unsalted butter, melted
10 phyllo sheets

Preheat the oven to 425°.

Place the chicken pieces, seasoned salt, and flour in a 1-quart plastic bag. Close the bag and shake until the chicken pieces are coated.

Over medium-high heat, bring the oil to bubbling in a small sauté pan. Place the chicken pieces in the pan and sauté until the juices no longer run pink, about 5 minutes. Transfer the chicken to a warm plate and keep it warm.

Reduce the heat to medium. Whisk the mustard into the chicken drippings. Add the tarragon and reduce slightly. Whisk in the cream, blending it all thoroughly. Reduce the heat to low and simmer until the sauce is reduced by one fourth. Add the chicken to sauce, remove from the heat, and set aside.

Brush a shallow 1-quart casserole with melted butter. Lay 1 phyllo sheet in the casserole, patting to fit sides. Brush it down with the melted butter. Repeat the process with 4 more phyllo sheets. Fill the casserole with the chicken mixture. Layer 5 more phyllo sheets on top of chicken, buttering between each sheet.

Trim excess phyllo to within 1 inch of dish edge. Tuck the phyllo edges under and brush with butter.

Bake for 15 minutes, or until top is crisply browned.

Emmy's Elegant Vegetable Medley

Vegetables are quite popular in Hollywood— they're good for you and they don't cost all that much for those Cary Grant and Madonna wanna-bes on a shoestring. This particular recipe looks quite complex but is really just a clever melding of ingredients.

MARINADE:
1/8 cup rice wine vinegar
1/3 cup balsamic vinegar
1/3 cup peanut oil
1 clove garlic, minced
1/2 teaspoon salt
1/2 teaspoon sugar
1/2 teaspoon dried oregano, crumbled
1/2 teaspoon dried basil, crumbled
Freshly ground black pepper to taste

VEGETABLES:
3/4 cup fresh broccoli florets, steamed and drained
1/8 cup chopped onion
1/4 pound mushrooms, thinly sliced
1/2 cup baby carrots, steamed and cut in half diagonally
7 ounces frozen artichoke hearts
1/4 cup ripe olives, sliced
1/4 cup sliced celery
1 ounce pimiento, drained and chopped

In a small saucepan, combine all the marinade ingredients over medium heat. Heat to boiling, reduce flame, then simmer uncovered for 10 minutes.

In a medium bowl, combine the onion, mushrooms, carrots, artichoke hearts, celery, olives, and pimiento. Pour the hot marinade over the vegetables and stir to coat. Cover and chill for several hours.

In a small bowl, marinate the broccoli by itself, then mix it in just before serving. It will hold its green color better if left alone!

Drain off the marinade before serving.

TIPS

❦ In Hollywood you can carry out any kind of food. Get a couple of Chinese carryout boxes and put sexy lingerie in them.

❦ Following through on this theme, customize your own fortune cookies! Lucky Duck Fortune Cookies will personalize fortune cookies for you—their number is 1-617-389-3583. This is a good way for shy folk to propose, or for passing on that important news of impending patter of little feet!

Perfect Picnics

ROMANTIC OPEN-AIR MENUS

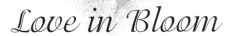

Love in Bloom

Vichyssoise
Chilled Asparagus Vinaigrette
Chicken Salad Amandine
Chocolate Truffles
Champagne

This light, delectable picnic is best complemented by champagne. You may choose to serve it plain, with a slice of strawberry dropped in for decoration, or you may flavor it into either a kir royale (add a splash of Chambord or raspberry liqueur) or a mimosa as made at Harry's Bar in Venice, Italy. (1 part orange juice, 1 part tangerine juice, and 3 parts champagne). Alternatively, you may serve a crisp dry wine, such as sauvignon blanc or soave classico. If you'd rather not serve alcohol, try a mild, dry ginger ale or a seltzer spritzer with lemon or lime. No matter which you serve, a silver champagne bucket with ice is always an elegant accent on the table.

"It was a lover and his lass
with a hey, and a ho, and a hey nonino
that o'er the green cornfield did pass,
In the spring time, the only pretty ring time,
When birds do ding, hey ding a ding, ding;
Sweet lovers love the spring."

—WILLIAM SHAKESPEARE,
As You Like It

Vichyssoise

Yukon gold potatoes are a good choice for this soup, as they give it a lovely golden color and taste naturally buttery. They're a little more expensive, but worth it.

Nondairy cream or plain yogurt can be used in place of the heavy cream in this recipe.

1 pound potatoes, peeled and chopped
2 leeks, washed and sliced (white part only)
1 tablespoon butter
4 cups chicken stock
1 cup milk
1 cup heavy cream
Salt
Pepper
Nutmeg
Chives

Sauté the potatoes and leeks in the butter, stirring often, for 15 minutes, or until tender. Do not brown.

Add the stock, cover, and simmer for 15 to 20 minutes.

Transfer the vegetables and stock into a blender and puree, adding the milk and cream slowly. Return the mixture to the pan and add salt, pepper, and nutmeg to taste.

Chill and garnish with chopped chives.

Chilled Asparagus Vinaigrette

Hazelnut oil is a mild, fruity oil easily found in grocery or gourmet stores. You may, if you prefer, use extra-virgin olive oil. Rice wine vinegar is available in the international section of most grocery stores, but you may use an excellent quality red wine vinegar instead.

$1/5$ cup chopped shallots
2 tablespoons vinegar
4 teaspoons hazelnut oil
1 tablespoon rice wine vinegar
2 teaspoons country Dijon mustard (or to taste)
1 teaspoon dried tarragon
8 to 10 stalks asparagus

Steam the asparagus until they're bright green and yield to the touch of a fork (about 10 minutes).

Meanwhile, combine the remaining ingredients in a blender and mix.

Pour vinegar mixture over cooked asparagus, chill and serve.

Chicken Salad Amandine

This chicken salad is really something special. The recipe is easily doubled or tripled to serve at a summer party, and the raves you will get for it will be most gratifying. Pineapple is the secret ingredient that no one will guess. Don't worry that it may overwhelm the chicken salad with sweetness—it won't. But feel free to play with the proportions; it's nearly impossible to go wrong.

Almost any sliced or chopped nut can be substituted for the almond, and we have had excellent results using chopped honey-roasted peanuts.

1 large skinless boneless chicken breast, halved
Seasoning salt
¹/₁ cup chopped pineapple
2 tablespoons Miracle Whip salad dressing
1 tablespoon mayonnaise
2 tablespoons sour cream (regular, light, or fat-free)
3 tablespoons sliced almonds
Salt
Freshly ground pepper
2 fresh croissants, sliced in half

Preheat oven to 350°.

Sprinkle the chicken breast liberally with the seasoning salt of your choice. Bake for about 25 minutes, or until cooked through.

Combine pineapple, Miracle Whip, mayonnaise, sour cream, almonds, salt, and pepper in a bowl. Season to taste.

Chill the chicken breasts so they're cool enough to chop, then toss the chicken in the dressing mix. Chill for at least an hour, then spread half of the mixture on each croissant.

Bon appétit!

TIPS

❦ A traditional basket with a red-and-white checked table-cloth is the perfect accessory to this meal. Wrap the utensils in linen napkins and tie with ribbon. A love note can easily be slipped between the folds.

❦ Another fun way to pack your picnic is to get two cake boxes from a bakery and pack each lunch individually. Tie the boxes with satin ribbon.

❦ The music of Edith Piaf sets a beautiful mood for this picnic.

Afternoon Delight

RT's BBQ Pork Sandwiches
Creamy Coleslaw
Copper Pennies
Almond Cookies
Iced Almond Tea

In a tucked-off section of Arlington, Virginia, sits the intimate confines of RT's Restaurant. It's known far and wide for its delicious Cajun cuisine and easygoing attitude. Many an afternoon is spent in the booths over lunches like this one—exchanging confidences, dreams, and lifetime plans.

"Oh, promise me that some day you and I
Will take our love together to some sky
Where we can be alone and faith renew,
And find the hollows where those flowers grew".

—CLEMENT WILLIAM SCOTT, *"Oh, Promise Me"*

RT's BBQ Pork Sandwiches

Whether you prefer spicy hot or sweet barbecue, you haven't tasted heaven until you've tasted Jim Cernak's barbecue! As chef at the romantic RT's Restaurant, Jim shares a favorite BBQ recipe with us.

PORK TENDERLOIN:

1/2 pound pork tenderloin
1 teaspoon salt
1 teaspoon dark brown sugar
1 teaspoon sugar
1 teaspoon ground cumin
1 teaspoon garlic powder
1 teaspoon ground black pepper
1/2 teaspoon cayenne pepper
2 teaspoons paprika
2 sandwich buns, split

Preheat the oven to 475°.

Mix the sugar and spices together in a small bowl until well blended. Pat the tenderloin with it, until completely coated.

Roast the tenderloin on a roasting rack for 15 minutes at 475°. Reduce the heat to 325° and roast for an additional 20 minutes. Remove from heat and let it stand for 15 minutes.

With two forks, pull the pork into thin shreds and set it aside.

BBQ SAUCE:

7/8 cup cider vinegar
5/8 cup peanut oil
5/8 cup fresh lemon juice
1/4 pound dark brown sugar
13 ounces ketchup
2 ounces Dijon mustard
1 1/2 teaspoons Coleman's English mustard
1 1/2 teaspoons Tabasco
1/2 cup Worcestershire sauce
2 1/4 teaspoons garlic, minced
1/4 cup Jack Daniel's Green

In a medium saucepan over medium-high heat, whisk together the oil, vinegar, lemon juice, brown sugar, ketchup, Dijon and Coleman mustards, Worcestershire sauce, and garlic. Bring all this to a boil, reduce the heat to low. Add the bourbon and simmer for 2 hours.

Reduce the sauce by one third.

Add 3/4 cup pulled pork to 1 cup BBQ sauce in a small sauté pan and reduce sauce by half.

Put the hot BBQ into a widemouthed thermos to keep it warm. Serve on split buns.

TIP

❧ John Mahoney, the daytime bartender at RT's, swears by these musical offerings: "Anything by B. B. King or Robert Cray."

Creamy Coleslaw

There is nothing quite like the creaminess of a slightly sweet, slightly vinegar-y coleslaw to top off and bring out the full flavor of a good BBQ!

¼ cup peanut oil
¼ cup rice wine vinegar
¼ teaspoon salt
¼ cup sugar
¼ teaspoon celery seed
¼ teaspoon salt
½ large carrot
½ medium onion, shredded
¼ head green cabbage, shredded
1 tablespoon sweet pickle relish

In a small saucepan over medium heat, bring the oil, vinegar, sugar, and celery seed to a boil, and boil for 1 minute. Remove the saucepan from the heat and let it cool to the touch.

Combine the shredded cabbage and vegetables; add the salt and the dressing mixture. Put it in your best Tupperware and chill for at least 4 hours.

Copper Pennies

This is a decades-old recipe that has graced many a romantic picnic. Its sweet tomato-y taste is addicting, and the longer you let it marinate in the refrigerator, the fuller the flavor.

1 cup carrots, scraped and cut into ¼-inch rounds
½ cup onion, diced large
½ cup green peppers, diced large
⅓ cup tomato soup
⅛ cup sugar
¼ cup rice wine vinegar
⅛ cup peanut oil
1 teaspoon country Dijon mustard
½ teaspoon Worcestershire sauce
Salt and freshly ground black pepper to taste

Bring a small pot of water to a boil over medium heat. Add the carrot rounds and boil for 5 minutes. Drain and set aside.

In a small bowl mix the onion, pepper, soup, sugar, vinegar, oil, mustard, Worcestershire sauce, and salt and pepper. When this has a copper velvet shine, add the carrots. Marinate for at least 4 hours, or overnight.

Autumn Memory

Cream of Cheddar Cheese Soup
Roast Beef French Dip
Roasted Chestnuts
Apples and Caramel
Hot Buttered Rum

Bundle up and take this picnic outdoors on a crisp autumn day. You can even bring it along to a football game.

The soup and hot buttered rum must be kept warm in thermoses, but the roasted chestnuts will stay warm enough wrapped in several layers of aluminum foil. The roast beef sandwiches will also stay warm in aluminum, or you may choose to eat them cold. Carry the jus in a small plastic container with a lid. Serve any kind of red wine with the roast beef sandwiches.

"I love all that thou lovest,
Spirit of Delight:
The fresh Earth in new leaves dressed,
And the starry night;
Autumn evening and the morn,
When the golden mists are born."

—PERCY BYSSHE SHELLEY, "Song"

Cream of Cheddar Cheese Soup

Carry this smooth, luscious soup in a thermos and serve it piping hot at your picnic.

If you want a sharper flavor, add more mustard.

1/4 cup unsalted butter
2 stalks celery, scrubbed and finely chopped
1/2 cup sliced leeks, white part only
1/2 cup flour
1 teaspoon dry mustard powder
Salt and freshly ground black pepper to taste
1 cup chicken or vegetable stock
1/2 cup table cream
1 cup milk
3/4 cup shredded cheddar cheese

Melt the butter or margarine in a heavy saucepan over medium heat. Add the celery and leeks. Simmer, stirring frequently, for 15 minutes, or until the vegetables are tender.

Add the flour, mustard, salt, pepper, and chicken stock. Simmer, stirring constantly, until mixture is thick (about 5 minutes), then slowly add the cream and milk. Cover and simmer 10 minutes, stirring occasionally. Reduce the heat to low and slowly add the cheese, stirring to a smooth consistency. Serve.

Roast Beef French Dip

These sandwiches can be served hot or cold, as can the au jus dip, depending on your preference. If you want to serve them hot on your picnic, wrap the hot meat in two layers of aluminum foil and bring the dip in a plastic container.

Mini baguettes, sliced lengthwise, are good for these sandwiches, but if you want to be decadent, you may use croissants.

1/2 pound roast
1 envelope onion soup mix
1 tablespoon flour
1 small oven cooking bag

Preheat the oven to 350°.

Combine all ingredients in an oven cooking bag. Hold one end of the bag and shake it until everything is mixed well. Seal the end and make several slits in the bag to prevent bursting. Place in a shallow baking dish and bake at 350° for 3 hours or more (up to about 5), according to your preference.

When the roast is done, save the juices from the bottom of the roasting pan—this is your au jus dip.

Slice the cooked roast thick or thin according to your preference and serve in sandwiches.

Light Love

ROMANTIC MENUS WITHOUT THE FAT

Divine Decadence

Yellow Split Pea Soup
Angel Hair Pasta with Braised Garlic
Roasted Garlic
Light Pesto
Italian Bread
Chocolate Kahlúa Soufflé
Lemon Spritzers

This meal offers some of the best food you can offer—that it is light is a pleasant side note. From the rich, thick soup to the satisfying pasta right down to the soufflé, you won't believe you're eating healthy!

Pick up a loaf of fresh Italian or French bread, or indeed any other favorite, for your garlic and pesto spreads. Italian holds up well to the spreading yet doesn't have a too-tough crust.

A crisp, dry white wine, like Soave Bolla, is a nice addition to this meal. The more calorie-conscious might prefer to make spritzers of half wine and half plain seltzer.

"Better is a dinner of herbs where love is . . ."
—PROVERBS

Yellow Split Pea Soup

You can use green split peas instead of yellow for this soup, but yellow tends to make a more appetizing color.

Also, you might like to crumble a slice of crisp turkey bacon over each bowl for flavor. While this will add calories, it will not add nearly as much as regular pork bacon.

1/3 cup yellow split peas
2 cups water
1 1/4 cups fat-free chicken broth
1 medium onion, chopped
2 cloves garlic, crushed
1 tablespoon flour
Salt and freshly ground black pepper to taste

Put the peas into a saucepan with the water and let them simmer 40 to 50 minutes, or until tender; then puree them.

Heat the chicken broth in the rinsed out saucepan and cook the onion for 10 minutes, or until it's transparent. Stir in the garlic and flour. Cook for a minute or two, then gradually pour in the split pea puree, stirring until you have a smooth mixture. Let the soup simmer 5 to 10 minutes and then season to taste.

Serve.

Angel Hair Pasta with Braised Garlic

This is best with angel hair or vermicelli, but those pastas stick quickly so you may want to prepare and serve over either linguine or fettucine—which tastes great too!

I recommend a flavorful, sharp grated cheese such as Pecorino romano because a tablespoon delivers a lot of flavor without the fat.

1/2 pound pasta
2 heads garlic, chopped
1/4 cup chicken stock
1 tablespoon balsamic vinegar
2 teaspoons light brown sugar
Salt, pepper, or other seasoning salt
Pecorino or Locatelli romano cheese, grated

Set salted water to boil for pasta in a large stockpot.

Meanwhile, heat half the chicken stock in a large pan over medium flame and add the garlic. Cook for 15 minutes, adding the rest of the stock slowly, as it thickens. Stir vinegar, brown sugar, and seasoning into the garlic mixture. If it's too thick to pour, add more stock or water.

Cook the pasta according to directions, drain it, and transfer to a large bowl. Add the sauce, toss, and garnish with cheese.

Roasted Garlic

This is a wonderful alternative to butter because it spreads easily on bread and imparts a lot of flavor.

1 head of garlic
1 teaspoon olive oil
1 pinch salt

Heat the oven to 350°.

Cut the top off a head of garlic so the cloves are exposed.

Drizzle oil on the garlic and sprinkle salt over it.

Wrap the garlic tightly in aluminum foil and bake for 40 minutes.

The garlic is ready to spread!

Light Pesto

You may spread this on bread, along with the roasted garlic, but it's also nice mixed in with the pasta and braised garlic.

1 cup fresh basil leaves
1 tablespoon fresh lemon juice
2 tablespoons toasted walnuts or pine nuts
5 cloves garlic, peeled and minced
Salt and freshly ground black pepper to taste
2 teaspoons olive oil
3 tablespoon grated Pecorino romano cheese
Enough water to make a smooth consistency

Combine all ingredients in a blender or food processor.

Chill and serve.

Chocolate Kahlúa Soufflé

1/4 cup granulated sugar
1/4 cup cocoa
1 tablespoon cornstarch or arrowroot
3/4 cup evaporated skim milk
2 tablespoons Kahlúa
3 eggs, separated, plus 1 egg white
1/4 teaspoon cream of tartar
2 tablespoons confectioners' sugar

Combine granulated sugar, cocoa, and cornstarch or arrowroot in the top of a double boiler. Stir in the Kahlúa and evaporated skim milk very slowly, so the mixture thickens.

Lightly beat 3 egg yolks. Stir a little of the hot mixture into the yolks, then transfer the entire mixture to the double boiler and cook over boiling water for 10 minutes, or until the mixture thickens. Remove from the heat and let it cool slightly.

Preheat the oven to 350°.

Beat all 4 egg whites and the cream of tartar until it forms stiff peaks. Add confectioners' sugar.

Fold egg whites into cooled chocolate mixture and put the entire mixture into a small ungreased soufflé dish.

Bake for 50 minutes, or until a strand of raw spaghetti inserted comes out clean.

Serve immediately.

Lemon Spritzers

This is a nice palate refresher after all that garlic!

20 ounces plain seltzer
2 teaspoons fresh lemon juice
2 teaspoons honey

For each glass of seltzer (about 10 ounces), add 1 teaspoon lemon juice and 1 teaspoon honey. Serve chilled and sip with straws.

TIPS

❧ If you'd like to have breadsticks instead of bread slices, rumple a paper bag to make it look "relaxed," then turn the edges down and line it with a pretty scarf or bandanna. Put the breadsticks in as a centerpiece. They're fun to dip in pesto and roasted garlic paste.

❧ James Galway's *Nocturnes* album is perfect with this meal.

Roman Holiday

Parmesan Tomatoes
Parslied Rice
Veal Piccata
Pesto Zucchini
Italian Rolls
Raspberry Torta
Sparkling Mineral Water

In days past, Italian food evoked images of all sorts of mouthwatering cream sauces, pasta and veal kissed with olive oil and spices, and dry red wine flowing like water. And all calorie-free, if—and only if—someone else ate it.

With a little imagination and creativity, the new Italian cuisine sings a song of gastronomical delight, while gently reminding us that taste is but a frame of mind, and calories can be watched with pleasure.

There are a wide variety of sparkling mineral waters on the market these days. Make sure you read the label and that any added flavoring is minus the fat and calories.

"How silver-sweet sound lovers' tongues by night,
Like softest music to attending ears!"

—WILLIAM SHAKESPEARE, Romeo and Juliet

Parmesan Tomatoes

You can buy Parmesean cheese by the piece or pregrated in a plastic tub. Of course, grating it just before you use it is the preferred way to fully experience its sharp, nutty flavor.

Romano cheese made in the United States from cow's milk can be substituted for Parmesan. But NEVER substitute the Italian-made Pecorino romano if the recipe calls for Parmesan— the pungent taste of this sheep's milk cheese is too strong!

Vegetable cooking spray
1 large ripe tomato, sliced 1" thick
1 teaspoon finely minced shallots
1¹/₂ teaspoons minced fresh oregano
2 teaspoons grated Parmesan cheese
1 teaspoon extra-virgin olive oil

Preheat broiler.
    Spray a shallow glass cooking dish with the cooking spray and place the tomato slices in a single layer.
    Combine the shallots, oregano, and cheese in a small bowl. Sprinkle this mixture over the tomato slices. Drizzle each tomato slice with olive oil.
    Broil 3 inches from heat for 3 to 5 minutes, until the cheese begins to brown.

Parslied Rice

When a more distinct grain of rice is preferred—such as for salads, side dishes, and curries—most cooks look to long-grain rice.

Whenever you cook rice, cover it tightly and cook it in the amount of liquid called for (usually water or broth) until all the liquid is absorbed and the rice is tender. DO NOT lift the lid on the pot until you are sure the rice is done. Then, remove the rice from the stove, let it stand for 5 minutes, and fluff with a fork before serving. Perfect every time!

Vegetable cooking spray
1/8 cup chopped onion
1/2 clove garlic, crushed
2/3 cup chicken broth
1/3 cup uncooked long-grain white rice
1 teaspoon chopped fresh parsley
Salt to taste

Coat a small saucepan with cooking spray and place over medium-high flame until hot (not smoking).
    Add the onion and garlic, cover, and cook until transparent, about 5 minutes. Add the rice and cook for 1 minute, stirring constantly. Stir in the broth, parsley, and salt.
    Bring to a boil; reduce the heat to medium, and simmer 15 to 20 minutes, or until all liquid is absorbed and the rice is tender.

Veal Picatta

Veal is always cooked through, so the timing for sautéeing is determined only by the thickness of the meat. The cutlets in this recipe are fairly thin (¼ inch), so they are best cooked over a medium-high heat. If you want to prepare a cutlet for scallopine, press gently to smooth it out, rather than pounding it as you would a heavier cut of beef. Pounding renders the veal cutlet dry, lifeless, and reminiscent of mystery meat meals served in college dining halls.

Sautéed veal cutlets invite the flavors of an accompanying sauce, such as this light lemon, sherry, and caper combination.

½ pound veal cutlets (¼ inch thick)
⅛ cup flour
Vegetable cooking spray
½ teaspoon extra virgin olive oil
¼ cup dry sherry
⅛ cup fresh lemon juice
1 tablespoon capers, small
1 tablespoon chopped fresh parsley
4 thin slices lemon

Trim any fat from cutlets and dredge them in flour. Coat a small nonstick sauté pan with the cooking spray, add the oil, and place over medium-high flame until hot (not smoking). Add veal and cook for 3 minutes on each side, or until browned. Remove the veal from pan and drain. Transfer the veal to a plate and put in low oven to keep warm.

Add the sherry, lemon juice, and capers to the pan and whisk, scraping up the brown bits from bottom of pan. Stir constantly until mixture is reduced by half; add the parsley.

Return the cutlets to the pan and heat through.

Place the cutlets on plates, pour sauce over them, and garnish with lemon slices.

Tips

❦ "Bistro" it up with a checkered tablecloth, red candles, and the addition of a carafe of alcohol-free white wine. Serve the food at table.

❦ For ultimate elegance, bring on the white linen, silver, china, crystal, and fresh-cut white roses. Plate the food in the kitchen so that the table has room to spare for handholding.

❦ Carreras, Domingo, and Pavarotti's *The Three Tenors in Concert 1994* is the perfect garnish for this romantic dinner.

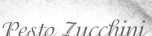

Pesto Zucchini

Locally grown zucchini is available in late summer from your grocery store and roadside stands—not to mention the never-ending supply that seems to appear in the office, courtesy of the weekend gardeners.

Cook zucchini only until it is tender—soft enough to yield slightly when pierced by a fork. This nutritious way of transporting the goodness of the garden to your table is also the tastiest way to bring out the natural flavors.

1 cup zucchini, unpeeled, cut into 2-inch-long strips
1 tablespoon extra-virgin olive oil
1 teaspoon chopped fresh basil
1 tablespoon grated Parmesan cheese
10 pine nuts
Salt and freshly ground black pepper to taste
3 fresh basil leaves

Place half of the olive oil in a small nonstick sauté pan. Add the zucchini and sauté for 4 minutes. Stir in the remaining ingredients and heat through.

Remove from the heat and serve, adding whole fresh basil leaves as garnish.

Raspberry Torta

What could be more romantic than the sweet-tartness of raspberries and cream enveloping the velvet touch of pound cake? Try feeding this to each other one light bite at a time—and take your time with the whipped topping!

Two $1/2$-inch slices of prepared fat-free pound cake
$2/3$ cup fresh raspberries
$1/4$ cup seedless raspberry jam
2 tablespoons water
1 dash almond extract
1 teaspoon toasted sliced almonds
Nonfat prepared whipped topping

Cube both slices of pound cake.

Heat raspberries, jam, water, and extract to bubbling in a small saucepan over medium flame.

Dividing the cake and mixture between two wineglasses, spoon a small bit of the raspberry mixture into each glass, add the cake cubes, and pour remaining fruit mixture over top.

Garnish with the nonfat whipped topping and sliced almonds.

Sweet Amore

Marinated Tomato Salad
Green Beans with Scallions
Cheesy Chicken Rolls
Fruit Clouds
Raspberry Seltzer

It's Thursday night. Tomorrow night is Friday. The kids are having a quality-time overnighter with Nana and Grandpa, the cat is going to kitty-camp, and you're leaving all the work you should do over the weekend at the office.

Friday night, it's just you and the object of your heart's desire.

Prepare this meal in its entirety on Thursday night when the household is in concert with the sandman. Come Friday night, dinner won't be the only thing you'll heat up . . .

"How do I love thee? Let me count the ways.
I love thee to the depth and breadth and height
My soul can reach, when feeling out of sight
For the ends of Being and ideal Grace."

—ELIZABETH BARRETT BROWNING,
"How Do I Love Thee?"

Marinated Tomato Salad

This salad is infused with the flavors and bouquet of fresh herbs. Basil is beautifully fragrant, and has an affinity for tomatoes. Oregano's spicy tendencies especially complement tomatoes. Tarragon (use the French, not the Russian—it's too coarse and undeveloped for cooking) has an aniselike flavor and traditionally flatters summer food.

Let this salad set overnight in the refrigerator to fully develop the herbal flavor blend!

1 1/2 teaspoons fresh basil, chopped
3/4 teaspoon fresh oregano, chopped
1/2 teaspoon fresh tarragon, chopped
1/4 cup balsamic vinegar
1/4 teaspoon Dijon mustard
3/4 cup tomatoes, thinly sliced
1 sweet onion (Vidalia if available), sliced paper thin
1 1/2 tablespoons extra-virgin olive oil
4 romaine lettuce leaves

In a small bowl, whisk together the herbs, vinegar, mustard, and oil to make a vinaigrette.

Place the tomatoes and onion in a single layer on a plate, and pour the vinaigrette over the vegetables.

Chill overnight and serve over the romaine lettuce leaves.

Green Beans with Scallions

Cooking green vegetables in water is a good news, bad news proposition. *Boiling* them in a large uncovered volume of water preserves their colors, but nutrients leach out. This is minimized when vegetables are *steamed*— cooked in a small amount of water in a covered pan—but the green colors simply are not as bright. So the choice of cooking methods is yours.

1/3 pound fresh green beans
1/2 cup water for steaming (1 quart for boiling)
1 tablespoon scallions, finely chopped
Salt and freshly ground black pepper to taste

Wash the beans, trim the ends, and cut them into 1 1/2-inch pieces.

Bring the water to boil in a small saucepan. Place the beans into steamer basket and cover pan (toss directly into the saucepan and do not cover if boiling).

Steam for 15 minutes (boil for 5).

Drain, add the scallions, and season with salt and pepper.

Cheesy Chicken Rolls

This recipe combines the best of Italian fantasy food, at a fraction of the calories!

2 boneless chicken breast halves
4 uncooked lasagna noodles
Vegetable cooking spray
1 cup finely chopped fresh broccoli
1/2 cup low-fat cottage cheese
1/2 cup low-fat ricotta cheese
1 small egg
1 teaspoon chopped fresh chives
1 pinch ground nutmeg
1 pinch freshly ground black pepper
1 tablespoon reduced-calorie margarine
2 tablespoons flour
1 cup chicken broth
1/2 cup skim milk
1/2 teaspoon Dijon mustard
Paprika

Preheat the oven to 350°.

Place the chicken breasts in a foil envelope and bake for 30 minutes. Cool and chop finely.

Bring 3 quarts of water to a boil, add the lasagna noodles one at a time, and cook them for 8 minutes. (They will be parboiled.) Drain them under cold water until they are cool to touch; lay out on flat piece of aluminum foil.

Spray a small nonstick sauté pan with the vegetable spray. Add the broccoli and cook for 3 minutes.

Combine the chicken, broccoli, cottage cheese, ricotta, egg, chives, nutmeg, and pepper. Split the mixture into fourths.

Spread the mixture on each lasagna noodle. Roll up the noodles, starting at the short end. Place the filled rolls, seam side down, in glass baking dish, and set aside.

Melt the margarine in small nonstick sauté pan over medium-high heat. Add the flour and whisk for 1 minute. Whisk in chicken broth and milk, small amounts at a time, then add the mustard. Whisk constantly, until thickened. Pour sauce over rolls, and sprinkle with paprika. Cover dish with foil and bake 20 to 30 minutes.

Fruit Clouds

The addition of gelatin to a dessert gives it added body, but it must be used with care: too much and the confection is rubbery; too little and it droops.

The beauty of this recipe is its versatility—change the fruit juice and extract and you have a brand-new taste sensation! We start you off with a lime juice version.

¹/₂ envelope unflavored gelatin
¹/₄ cup water
2 tablespoons frozen limeade concentrate, thawed
1¹/₂ tablespoons Equal Measure
¹/₈ teaspoon lemon extract
³/₄ cup small ice cubes
1 egg white
¹/₈ teaspoon cream of tartar

Mix limeade concentrate and water in a small saucepan, then sprinkle in the gelatin. Heat over low flame, whisking constantly, until the gelatin is dissolved.

Remove from the heat and whisk in the Equal and lemon extract. Add the ice cubes and whisk until mixture thickens. Discard any remaining pieces of ice. Set aside.

Beat the egg white and cream of tartar until stiff. Fold the limeade mixture into the egg white gently and thoroughly.

Put in wineglasses and chill at least 1 hour before serving.

TIPS

❧ For perfect pasta, allow the water to reach a vigorous boil before adding the pasta. Add the noodles in small amounts so that the water does not cool and lose its boil. (If it does, cover the pot for a moment until the boil resumes.)

❧ Place the Cheesy Chicken Rolls on fat "mattresses" of parsley for a whimsical presentation.

❧ Begin to relax with tunes from Ol' Blue Eyes himself with *Frank Sinatra: A Man & His Music.*

From the Garden

ROMANTIC VEGETARIAN MENUS

Mediterranean Mélange

Soupe de Provence avec Pistou
Sun-Dried Tomato Fougasse
Roasted Summer Peppers and Tomatoes with Cheese
Tapenade / Creamy Olive Spread
Steamed Baby Carrots with Parsley
Light Chianti

For this menu, we move to another part of the Mediterranean; back to the land of Princess Grace and, more recently, Peter Mayle. This Provençal dinner is an inspired idea for a sultry, lazy summer evening.

You need to serve a vigorous red wine with this. If you can find a Provençal red, so much the better, although light chianti is unusually delicious with this particular combination of foods (hence we have broken the French mood with an Italian wine!). Other alternatives include dolcetto or zinfandel.

"My vegetable love should grow
Vaster than empires, and more slow."

—ANDREW MARVELL, "To His Coy Mistress"

Soupe de Provence avec Pistou

This soup is a harmonious blend of Provençal vegetables and makes a lovely dinner for a summer evening on the terrace.

S O U P :
2 tablespoons olive oil
4 cloves garlic, peeled and minced
2 onions, peeled and chopped
1 leek (white part only), sliced
1 turnip, peeled and chopped
1 parsnip, peeled and chopped
1 carrot, peeled and chopped
1/2 cup peeled and chopped summer squash
3 potatoes, peeled and chopped
3/4 cup torn Swiss chard leaves (about 5 leaves)
2 tomatoes, blanched, peeled, and chopped (or 1 cup crushed)
1/2 cup cooked cannellini or garbanzo beans
Salt and freshly ground black pepper to taste
1/4 cup snipped fresh basil, parsley, and sage
2 1/2 cups water

Heat the olive oil in a medium saucepan and sauté the garlic, onions, leek, turnip, parsnip, and carrot, for 10 minutes over medium-low heat, or until the onion becomes limp and transparent.

Add the squash, potatoes, tomatoes, beans, and water. Simmer for at least an hour, but preferably all day (it will make the house smell delicious).

During the last 20 minutes of simmering, add the herbs, salt, and pepper.

Garnish with Pistou, serve.

P I S T O U :

This is really just a creamy pesto; if you refer, you can use the traditional basil pesto or the Light Pesto (see page 48).

For this dish, the milder parmigiano-reggiano is better than the sharp Pecorino or Locatelli romano, but this is one instance in which you can use either—or a combination of both.

1 cup basil leaves
4 cloves garlic, peeled and minced
1/2 cup grated Parmesan or romano cheese
1/2 cup crème fraîche
Freshly ground black pepper to taste

Combine all the ingredients except the crème fraîche in a blender or food processor and process on high for 30 seconds.

Turn the processor to low and add the crème fraîche in a slow steady stream.

Add pepper to taste and chill for 1 hour before serving.

Sun-Dried Tomato Fougasse

This flat Provençal bread is very much like Italian focaccia and is a fine addition to any Italian meal as well.

5 pieces sun-dried tomato
1/4 cup boiling water
1/2 cup whole milk
1 tablespoon butter
2 cups flour
1 package dry yeast
1 tablespoon sugar
1 teaspoon salt
1 small egg
2 teaspoons chopped dried chives
2 tablespoons olive oil
1/4 teaspoon oregano
1/4 teaspoon rosemary

Preheat the oven to 350°.

Combine the sun-dried tomato pieces and boiling water in a saucepan and let sit for 30 minutes, then drain, reserving the liquid in the pan. Set the tomato pieces aside.

Add the milk and butter to the "tomato water" in the saucepan, heat to warm.

Combine 3/4 cup of flour, yeast, sugar, and salt in a bowl and slowly stir in the milk, butter, and tomato-water mixture. Add the egg and chopped chives and mix thoroughly.

Finally, add the rest of the flour, enough to make a smooth, elastic loaf. Knead for 10 minutes.

Put the bread in a greased bowl, cover, and let rise for 1 hour or until doubled in bulk. Punch it down and press all the air out.

Shape the dough into a flattish circle and put it on a greased pan. Let it rise for 10 minutes.

Combine olive oil, oregano, and rosemary and brush half the mixture onto the risen loaf.

Bake for 15 minutes, brush on the remaining oil and herb mixture, then bake 5 to 10 minutes more, or until the loaf sounds hollow when you tap on it.

TIPS

❧ A wine bottle candleholder with a dripping candle in it may be an old idea, but it's still a romantic one. The informality of this meal calls for that sort of casual touch.

❧ The soundtrack from *Charade* by Henry Mancini is just the thing to put anyone into a French mood. The music is from the romantic movie of the same name starring Audrey Hepburn and the Romantic Lead himself, Cary Grant.

Roasted Summer Peppers with Tomatoes and Cheese

You may use red, yellow, green, or purple peppers for this appetizer, but sweet red peppers are a personal favorite.

2 tablespoons olive oil
1 tablespoon balsamic vinegar
2 large red bell peppers, halved and seeded
1 large ripe tomato
$^1/_4$ pound fresh mozzarella cheese
Salt and freshly ground black pepper to taste

Heat the broiler.

Place the halved peppers, skin side up, onto the broiling pan and broil for 5 to 7 minutes, or until the skin is blackened.

Remove the peppers to a bowl and cover quickly with a plate. Let them sit for 10 minutes, then remove the peppers from the bowl and peel the skins off.

Combine the oil and vinegar in a small bowl.

Place the peppers on a small, pretty serving plate and drizzle half of the oil and vinegar over them. Then place a slice of tomato and a slice of mozzarella on each pepper half and drizzle with the rest of the oil and vinegar mix.

Season with salt and pepper and serve.

Tapenade

This is fast and easy and makes a tasty spread for bread. If you prefer a creamier spread for your Fougasse, try the olive spread below.

$^1/_2$ cup black olives, pitted and chopped
4 cloves garlic, peeled and minced
1 tablespoon drained capers or 2 sardines
2 to 3 tablespoons olive oil, depending on preferred consistency
1 teaspoon fresh lemon juice
Salt to taste

Combine all the ingredients in a blender or food processor and process for 30 seconds, or until smooth.

Serve.

Creamy Olive Spread

You might want to make this instead of or in addition to Tapenade, for variety.

$^1/_2$ cup green olives, pitted (pimientos are okay)
4 ounces cream cheese
1 tablespoon whipping cream or milk

Combine all ingredients in a blender or food processor and puree to a smooth, thick consistency.

Serve.

Wintry Bisque Meal

Zucchini Bisque
Steamed Broccoli with Lemon Pepper
Cottage Cheese Salad
Whole Grain Bread
Ice-Cream Custard
Dry White Wine

It's amazing how delicate this simple bisque is, and your dinner companion
will have difficulty believing that the "secret ingredient" is zucchini.
(In some cases it's best not to tell!)

Make the bisque and bread, and your kitchen will smell divine—a quick
way to any man or woman's heart.

Ice-cream custard is the perfect happy ending to this very traditional meal,
because it's a direct lift from Grandmother's recipe box.

"Drink to me only with thine eyes,
And I will pledge with mine;
Or leave a kiss but in the cup
And I'll not look for wine."

—BEN JONSON, "To Celia"

Zucchini Bisque

This makes a smooth, thick bisque somewhat akin to potato and leek soup.

It's important to use a mild, preferably homemade vegetable stock. Nonvegetarians can use chicken stock instead of vegetable stock, if they prefer.

2 small zucchini (about 1 pound), peeled and shredded
1 small white onion, peeled and coarsely chopped
1/4 cup butter or margarine
1 cup vegetable stock
1/2 cup heavy cream (you may also use table cream or milk)
1/4 teaspoon each: nutmeg, salt, pepper, and dried crushed basil

Melt the butter in a large skillet and cook the onion until tender.

Add the zucchini and vegetable stock and simmer 20 minutes, or until limp.

Puree half of the batch at a time with spices and return entire mixture to a large pot over medium heat.

Stir in the cream and serve warm or cold.

Steamed Broccoli with Lemon Pepper

Lemon pepper is offered commercially at your local grocery store from a variety of vendors. The tang of its lemon properties combined with the spiciness of the pepper brings the steamed broccoli to a new life. The taste rivals the richness (and calories) of a hollandaise!

1/2 pound broccoli florets
1/2 cup water
1 tablespoon commercial lemon pepper

Bring the water to a roiling boil in a small saucepan; add the broccoli in a steamer tray. Cover and steam for 5 minutes, until bright green.

Remove to a serving dish or individual plates and toss with lemon pepper.

Cottage Cheese Salad

This simple little salad is nice served after the bisque and vegetable.

¹/₂ head of lettuce, washed and shredded -
¹/₂ cup cottage cheese
1 peach, peeled and sliced
1 banana, chopped

In two serving bowls, create a bed of lettuce and top with a scoop of cottage cheese.
Place slices of fruit on top.
Serve.

TIPS

❧ Zucchini bisque is wonderful served in "bread bowls." To do this, take the whole grain bread (or make or buy any sturdy bread), cut it in half, and hollow each side out, leaving about ³/₄ inch of bread. Trim down if the "bowls" are too tall. Ladle bisque into each and serve.

❧ If you serve this wintry meal in the summer—or even on a day when you're longing for summer—serve the ice cream in small clean ceramic planters, topped with edible mint or candied violets.

❧ The best music for this throwback meal is Frank Sinatra with the Tommy Dorsey Orchestra.

Ice-Cream Custard

This old-time recipe harkens back at least to the 1940s and probably farther than that. It's one of life's great simple pleasures.

1 teaspoon cornstarch or arrowroot
1 tablespoon sugar
1¹/₂ cups milk
¹/₂ cup semi-sweet chocolate chips
1 egg
1 cup evaporated milk

Blend the cornstarch and sugar in a small pot or double boiler, and heat over medium-low flame, slowly stirring in the milk and the chocolate.
Stir constantly until the chocolate has melted and the milk comes to a boil, thickening the mixture.
Remove from heat.
Crack the egg into a small bowl and beat lightly. Add some of the hot mixture to the egg, stirring immediately so that the egg doesn't cook.
Return the egg mixture to the hot mixture, stirring briskly.
Add the evaporated milk and allow the mixture to cool slightly, stirring frequently. Pour the entire mixture into a plastic container and freeze for at least 4 hours—preferably overnight.
Allow this custard to thaw slightly before serving.

Passion

Hummus and Torn Pita
Feta and Walnut Salad
Eggplant Obsession
Apple Tart
Royal Tomato Juice

Passion—that moment of recognition, when you realize that your heart, soul, and body have submitted to pure emotional desire. And from that moment, the commitment grows.

> *"Love is a growing, or full constant light,*
> *And his first minute after noon, is night."*

> —JOHN DONNE, "A Lecture Upon the Shadow"

Hummus and Torn Pita

Chickpeas, or garbanzo beans, have been world-class globe-trotters for centuries. They originated in Southwest Asia, moved to Sicily and Switzerland, then drifted around the Mediterranean, to India, and then to Brazil and Mexico.

One 15¹/₂-ounce can of chickpeas, drained
¹/₈ cup fresh lemon juice
1 tablespoon sesame oil
¹/₂ teaspoon minced garlic
1 dash Tabasco
2 small pita rounds, torn into bite-size pieces

Place all the ingredients in a blender or small food processor and process until the mixture is smooth and creamy. Remove the hummus to a serving bowl and refrigerate for at least 4 hours.

Note: this is one of those dishes that gets more flavorful overnight.
   Serve with the torn pita.

Feta and Walnut Salad

Feta cheese is synonymous with things Greek. It is slightly salty, can be made with cow's, sheep's, or goat's milk, and crumbles with gentle ease for cooking and salads.

SALAD:
3 cups fresh spinach, torn into bite-size pieces
¹/₂ small avocado, thinly sliced
¹/₂ small red onion, thinly sliced and separated
   into rings
¹/₄ cup crumbled feta cheese
¹/₄ cup chopped walnuts

In a small bowl, toss together all of the ingredients and set aside.

DRESSING:
¹/₈ cup balsamic vinegar
1 tablespoon finely chopped fresh basil
1 teaspoon honey
1 teaspoon Dijon mustard
¹/₂ teaspoon minced garlic
Salt and freshly ground black pepper to taste
¹/₄ cup peanut oil

In a small bowl, whisk together the vinegar, basil, honey, Dijon mustard, garlic, and salt and pepper. Slowly add the oil, whisking to emulsify the liquid.
   Pour the dressing onto the spinach-vegetable combination and toss gently.

Eggplant Obsession

It's a bold fruit, the eggplant. Its roots date back to the Middle Ages, when the Crusades introduced it to Europe from the Holy Land. Choose the best—glossy and uniformly purple. If the skin is dull or dotted with brown, it's past its prime.

1 small eggplant, peeled and thinly sliced
1 small onion, chopped
1/2 green pepper, chopped
1 tablespoon unsalted butter
1 tablespoon peanut oil
1/2 cup chopped oysters with juice
1/2 cup grated Monterey Jack cheese
1/2 cup small shrimp, cooked, peeled, and
    deveined
1/2 tablespoon flour
1/2 teaspoon freshly ground black pepper
1/2 teaspoon seasoned salt
1 pinch Beau Monde seasoning
1/4 cup fresh bread crumbs

Preheat oven to 350°.

Parboil the eggplant until fork-tender. Drain thoroughly and place on a plate.

In a small sauté pan, heat the butter and oil until hot, then add onion and pepper and sauté until tender.

In a small bowl, mix together the oysters, cheese, shrimp, flour, pepper, salt, and Beau Monde. Add in the eggplant and the onion-pepper mixture. If it's a little too dry, add a splash of half-and-half or a teaspoon of melted butter.

Put the mixture into a 2-quart baking dish and sprinkle with the bread crumbs. Bake for 45 minutes.

Royal Tomato Juice

A cool vegetable drink is the proper finish here. If you prefer, you can prepare it without the vodka—it remains just as exciting.

10 to 20 ice cubes
1 cup tomato juice
6 ounces lemon vodka
4 teaspoons fresh lemon juice
1/2 teaspoon horseradish
2 dashes Worcestershire sauce
2 dashes Tabasco
Freshly ground black pepper

Fill a mixing glass or pitcher with the ice cubes and add the tomato and lemon juices, lemon vodka, horseradish, Worcestershire sauce, and Tabasco. Season with a few grinds of black pepper.

Stir until mixed and cold, and pour into chilled 8-ounce glasses.

Apple Tart

Sometimes unusual tastes, as those set out in this menu, are nicely balanced by an American standard . . . the apple pie. These nicely sized tarts are just the ending for this unusual meal.

¹/₂ refrigerated Pillsbury piecrust
1 teaspoon flour
Vegetable cooking spray
1 medium apple (Mountaineer or Granny Smith are good), peeled and coarsely chopped
1 tablespoon unsalted butter, melted
¹/₈ cup chopped pecans
1 tablespoon light brown sugar
¹/₈ cup apricot preserves
¹/₂ teaspoon honey
2 dollops of créme fraîche

Preheat oven to 375°.

Let piecrust stand at room temperature for 15 minutes, then cut it in half.

Spray two 3-inch tart tins (with removable bottoms) with vegetable cooking spray and coat each with ¹/₂ teaspoon of flour. Place crust in each tart tin, easing the dough into the curves; cut off the excess dough with a knife. With a fork, poke holes on the sides and bottom of the tart dough. Bake the tarts for 10 minutes, then remove them from the oven and cool for 15 minutes.

Place the apples in the tart tins, brush the melted butter on top, then sprinkle with the sugar and pecans.

Bake for 30 minutes, until the apples are soft. Remove the tarts from the tin immediately.

In a small saucepan over medium-low heat, whisk the preserves and honey until warmed through.

Brush the apricot and honey mixture over the hot tarts.

A dollop of crème fraîche on top adds a rich taste to complement the sweetness of the honey glaze.

TIPS

❦ Put the dinner on, make a couple of Royal Tomatoes, pour a deep soaking bath—with bubbles—and both of you can relax together in the enveloping serenity of the water. Let the day's stresses slip quietly away while, for a moment, only the two of you exist, no one else.

❦ *Meditation: Classical Relaxation*—this boxed set of more than 10 hours of exquisite classics can help create an island of calm in your hectic life.

Songs of the Sea

ROMANTIC SEAFOOD MENUS

Scampi and Lemon Delight

Smooth Potato Soup
Shrimp Scampi
Wild Rice and Peas
Buttermilk Biscuits
Lemon Pudding
Homemade Lemonade

Shrimp scampi is, without a doubt, one of the most splendid dishes there is—so easy and yet so delicious. The combination of shrimp, garlic, wine, and butter gives new meaning to the word harmony.

We've started this meal with a mild, smooth potato soup to whet the appetite. Then comes the intense flavor of the scampi. The biscuits make for tasty punctuation with either plain or garlic butter. Lemon pudding is the only thing, apart from perhaps a lemon ice, that could follow this garlic and wine dish.

Serve with spritzers made of plain seltzer plus white Rhône, verdicchio, or frascati.

> "I will make you brooches and toys for your delight
> Of bird-song at morning and star-shine at night.
> I will make a place fit for you and me
> Of green days in forests and blue days at sea.
> I will make my kitchen and you shall keep your room
> Where white flows the river and bright blows the broom."

—ROBERT LOUIS STEVENSON, "The Vagabond"

Smooth Potato Soup

This mild soup is a perfect precursor to a flavorful meal like scampi.

Not to be confused with vichyssoise, this is a warm potato soup. It can be served with almost anything.

1 small onion, peeled and chopped
1 large potato, peeled and diced
1 tablespoon butter
3/4 cup milk
1 1/2 cups chicken stock or water
1 teaspoon salt
Freshly ground black pepper
Fresh chives

Melt the butter in a large saucepan and sauté the onions for 5 minutes, stirring often, until they're limp.

Add potato and cook another 2 to 3 minutes, then stir in the milk, water, and salt. Bring to a boil and simmer for 20 to 30 minutes, until vegetables are tender.

Puree the soup to a smooth consistency; then return it to the saucepan, heat it to warm, and season with salt and pepper.

Garnish with chives and serve.

Shrimp Scampi

You can use any size shrimp for this dish and the taste will be virtually the same. Small shrimp are a lot more work but they also tend to be considerably less expensive than the large or jumbo.

1 pound raw shrimp, peeled and deveined
1/2 cup butter or margarine
2 cloves garlic, minced
1/2 cup dry white wine (Chinese cooking wine is excellent)
1 tablespoon honey
1/2 teaspoon each: marjoram, basil, oregano
Salt and freshly ground black pepper to taste
2 cups cooked rice

Steam the shrimp for 3 to 5 minutes or until done, but not overdone.

Melt the butter in a large pan and add the wine, garlic, and seasoning. Cook over low-medium heat until the alcohol has burned off (10 minutes); add the shrimp, stir, and spoon over rice.

Serve.

Lemon Pudding

This pudding will separate when cooked, with a nice lemony sauce ending up on the bottom.

When grating the lemon rind, be careful not to get any of the bitter white part.

> *1 tablespoon unsalted butter*
> *1/4 cup fine sugar*
> *2 teaspoons grated fresh lemon rind*
> *1 tablespoon fresh lemon juice*
> *1 egg, separated*
> *1 pinch cream of tartar*
> *1/4 cup whole milk*
> *1/4 cup flour*

Preheat the oven to 350° and grease two custard cups.

Cream the butter with the sugar, then add the lemon rind, lemon juice, egg yolk, flour, and milk.

Whip the egg white with the cream of tartar until stiff peaks form, then fold it into the lemon mixture.

Pour half the mixture into each custard cup and place the custard cups in a pan of 1/2-inch water.

Bake for 30 to 35 minutes, or until the tops are golden brown.

Homemade Lemonade

Is there a better thirst-quencher than lemonade? We don't think so. It's a good idea to make lots of this because it inevitably gets consumed quickly.

> *2/3 cup sugar*
> *5 cups cold water*
> *Lemon peels from 2 lemons*
> *1 cup fresh lemon juice (about 10 lemons)*

In a saucepan, combine the sugar, 1 cup of water, and the lemon peels.

Simmer gently over medium heat for 8 minutes; set aside. When cool, strain the ingredients into a 2-quart serving pitcher. Add the fresh lemon juice and remaining water.

Stir in two trays of ice cubes and serve.

TIPS

❦ For this tropical meal, you might want to make place mats out of old maps, perhaps of places the two of you would like to travel to and explore together.

❦ Issue an invitation to dinner on what looks like airline tickets.

❦ James Galway's album *Song of the Seashore* is a lovely Japanese-inspired accompaniment to this meal.

Swordfish Symphony

Chilled Cucumber Soup
Swordfish with Lemon and Garlic
Twice-Baked Potatoes
Dutch Green Beans
Lemon Italian Ice
White Wine Spritzers

Swordfish has got to be one of the most universally appealing fishes there is—even those who don't normally like fish tend to be beguiled by a thick, buttery swordfish steak. Put some flavorful Twice-Baked Potatoes on the side and you will win even the most resistant heart.

Begin with a chilled cucumber soup that warms up the tastebuds gently without overwhelming. White wine spritzers will enhance, and not detract from, this meal, and can be made with any white wine, but we tend to prefer a dry or medium one to a sweet one with this meal—perhaps a sauvignon blanc, pinot grigio, muscadet sur lie, or chardonnay.

Wine spritzers are simply a combination of wine and seltzer water, usually in a fifty-fifty proportion.

"A livelier emerald twinkles in the grass,
A purer sapphire melts in the sea."

—ALFRED LORD TENNYSON, "Maud"

Chilled Cucumber Soup

This is a favorite summer soup, and it always receives raves. The cucumber, yogurt, and dill are a traditional Greek combination.

1 large cucumber, peeled and coarsely chopped
1 clove garlic, peeled and crushed in a little salt
2 cups plain yogurt
1/4 cup walnut pieces
Salt
Freshly ground black pepper
1 tablespoon chopped fresh dill or parsley (or 1 teaspoon dried dill and 2 teaspoons chopped fresh parsley)

In a blender or food processor, puree the cucumber, garlic, yogurt, walnuts, salt, and pepper. Blend until mixture becomes a smooth puree.

Chill thoroughly and serve garnished with chopped fresh dill or parsley.

TIPS

❦ Instead of serving the lemon ice in wineglasses, hollow out two orange halves and serve the ice in them.

❦ Gershwin's *Porgy and Bess* soundtrack goes nicely with this summertime menu.

Swordfish with Lemon and Garlic

This is an easy, easy dish but extremely elegant. Fresh swordfish can be expensive, but we've found excellent flash-frozen swordfish steaks at the local warehouse club.

Also, a sauce is unnecessary and many people prefer swordfish without it, but if you like hearty flavors, Tiger Sauce is a nice accompaniment.

2 swordfish steaks
6 garlic cloves, peeled and sliced
2 lemons
2 tablespoons butter
Freshly ground black pepper

Heat the broiler or grill.

Slice 3 long slits in each swordfish steak and push sliced garlic into them.

Cut 1 lemon in half and squeeze the juice from each half onto a swordfish steak.

Slice each tablespoon of butter into 3 pats and arrange on top of each swordfish steak.

Slice the other lemon and garnish each steak with 3 slices.

Top with pepper and broil for 10 minutes, or until cooked through or opaque.

Serve.

Twice-Baked Potatoes

If you have the confidence to try this, use a hand mixer on low speed to make a design in the potato after you've spooned the potato mixture back into the skins and are ready to bake for the second time.

1 large potato
1/2 cup sour cream or plain yogurt
1 egg
2 tablespoons butter
Any or all of the following potato toppers, in any amount: chives, bacon bits, shredded cheese, dried onion, pepper

Preheat oven to 450°.

Bake the potato at 450° for 1 hour. Remove from oven, slice in half lengthwise, and allow to cool for 10 minutes or so.

Remove the insides and put them in a mixing bowl, trying to keep the skin intact.

Mix the potato to smooth and add all other ingredients, saving the potato toppers for last. Add toppers and stir once or twice—enough to spread them throughout the mixture without grinding them in.

Spoon the mixture back into the potato skins. Reduce oven temperature to 350° and bake for 15 minutes, or until tops are lightly browned.

Serve.

Dutch Green Beans

Although we've devised this recipe with fresh green beans, frozen are perfectly fine in a pinch; stay away from canned, though—too salty!

1 cup fresh green beans (or 1/2 package frozen)
1 teaspoon unsalted butter
1/4 cup finely chopped onions
1/4 teaspoon Colman's dry English mustard
1/2 tablespoon balsamic vinegar
1 teaspoon bacon, cooked and crumbled
1 teaspoon light brown sugar
Salt and freshly ground black pepper to taste

In a small saucepan, boil the beans for 10 minutes, or until crispy-tender; drain them and set aside.

In a small sauté pan over medium heat, melt the butter. Add the onions and cook for about 10 minutes as well; reduce the heat to low.

In a cup, whisk together the mustard, vinegar, bacon, and brown sugar.

Add the seasonings and beans to the onions. Heat through and serve!

Remember Me

Tomato Aspic with Dill
Pleasantly Puffed Scallops
Sugar Snap Peas with Red Peppers
Dipping Cannoli
Gin Fizz

Simple things are for remembering love. The smell of the first chill day in autumn, the quiet of a snowfall, the crackle of a hot fire, a soft perfume, an aftershave lingering on the pillowcase.

This meal will bring back memories for you. It may be the creaminess of the scallops in puff pastry or it may be the fun of dipping the ends of your cannoli. Or it may be the sweet floral of the orange-blossom water in the Gin Fizz. Whatever it may be, cherish the moment, for it is unique in time.

"What ecstasies her bosom fire!
How her eyes languish with desire!"

—JOHN GAY,
"To a Lady on Her Passion for Old China"

Tomato Aspic with Dill

Aspic has long been celebrated for its complex blend of tastes and textures. This tomato aspic with dill stands in good company, along with hardier terrines and galantines, providing the special touch that elevates a meal to a higher level of elegance.

ASPIC:
3 tablespoons unflavored gelatin
1/4 cup cold water
1 1/4 cups spicy tomato juice
1 tablespoon grated onion
2 tablespoons finely chopped green pepper
1/4 cup finely chopped celery
1 teaspoon dillweed
1/4 teaspoon finely chopped fresh basil
1/4 teaspoon Worcestershire sauce
1/4 teaspoon salt
1/4 teaspoon sugar
1 tablespoon fresh lemon juice

In a small saucepan, sprinkle the gelatin over water and bring to a simmer over medium-high heat. Whisk in tomato juice and bring to a boil. Remove from the heat and let the mixture come to room temperature.

When cool, add onion, green pepper, celery, dill, basil, Worcestershire sauce, salt, sugar, and lemon juice. Pour mixture into a food processor and puree.

Pour into two well-oiled ceramic ramekins. Chill in refrigerator until set. Serve in or out of ramekins with the dressing.

DRESSING:
1/4 cup whipped cream cheese
1 teaspoon chopped green olives
1 dash of garlic powder
Half-and-half
2 sprigs of fresh dill

In a small food processor, mix the cream cheese and garlic until smooth. Add enough half-and-half to bring the dressing to a creamy consistency. Pulse in the olives.

Pour over the individual aspics and garnish each with a sprig of fresh dill.

Pleasantly Puffed Scallops

The succulent scallop is a bivalve member of the mollusk community. Distantly related to oysters, mussels, and clams, the larger sea scallop lives in the waters of the Atlantic Ocean; the smaller bay and calico scallops are known to frequent Atlantic estuaries and bays.

These sweet mouthfuls are harvested year-round, but unlike their hardier cousins, they are sold after they are shucked.

1 1/2 tablespoons peanut oil
2 tablespoons leek, julienned and cut into 1-inch
    lengths
2 tablespoons carrot, julienned and cut into
    1-inch lengths
2 tablespoons finely chopped celery
1/4 cup dry white wine
1/2 cup bay scallops, cut into thirds
1 tablespoon unsalted butter
1/2 teaspoon finely chopped fresh parsley
1/2 teaspoon minced garlic
Salt and freshly ground black pepper to taste
1 teaspoon white Worcestershire sauce
1/2 teaspoon cornstarch
1 tablespoon water
2 pastry shells

Bake pastry shells according to package directions.

In a small sauté pan, heat 1/2 tablespoon oil over medium-high flame until hot; sauté the leek, carrot, and celery for 1 minute. Add in the wine and simmer the mixture for 3 minutes. Set this aside and keep it warm.

Pat the scallops dry.

In another small sauté pan, heat 1 tablespoon oil and butter over medium-high flame until the butter melts; add the scallops and sauté until they are almost cooked, about 3 minutes. Add the parsley, garlic, salt, pepper, and the white Worcestershire sauce. Stir in the reserved vegetables and heat through.

Mix cornstarch and water and add to the scallop mixture; stir until slightly thickened.

Spoon into pastry shells, letting any extra to spill over the edges of the shells. Garnish with parsley sprigs and julienned carrots.

Sugar Snap Peas with Red Peppers

Sugar snap peas are a sweet combination of green beans and green peas. They are eaten in their entirety like beans or snow peas, as opposed to being shucked like peas. They may not be readily available in your local grocery store, but you will be able to find them at specialty food shops or produce stands.

1 tablespoon peanut oil
1/8 cup finely chopped onion
1 cup fresh sugar snap peas
1/2 sweet red pepper, cut into strips
1 teaspoon soy sauce
1 teaspoon sesame seeds, toasted
Salt and freshly ground black pepper to taste

Steam sugar snap peas for 3 minutes; drain and plunge into cold water to retard cooking.

In a small sauté pan, heat oil over medium-high flame until hot. Add onion and sauté until tender, about 5 minutes. Add sugar snap peas and red pepper, and sauté for an additional 2 or 3 minutes; add soy sauce, sesame seeds, and salt and pepper and heat through.

Serve in Oriental-style serving bowl.

Dipping Cannoli

2 plain cannoli

You and your dinner companion dip the ends of your cannoli in custard cups half full of one—or two—of the items below:

Mini chocolate bits
Crushed hazelnuts
Crushed pistachios
Crushed chocolate jimmies
Crushed toffee candy

TIPS

❦ Any of the "Hooked on Classics" recordings are perfect accompaniment for shaking the Gin Fizzes.

❦ Enclose snapshots of the two of you in stiff plastic sleeves to make coasters. Write "I love you" across the bottom of them in different languages:

❦ te amo—Spanish

❦ je t'aime—French

❦ ti amo—Italian

❦ Thaim in Grabh Leat—Gaelic

❦ Ich liebe dich—German

❦ Aloha Wau Ia Oe—Hawaiian

Bar and Grill

ROMANTIC BISTRO-STYLE MENUS

Lobster Celebration

Shrimp Cocktail
Jack Tarr Potatoes
Worcestershire-Grilled Lobster Tail
Buttered Snow Peas
Napoleons
Champagne

This is a lucky meal. Coauthor Elizabeth Harbison became engaged over this meal one summer night and has had no regrets since.

A word about napoleons: It's difficult to make them as well as real pastry chefs can, so don't bother. Buy them fresh from your favorite bakery.

Toasty/yeasty champagne, such as Moët et Chandon Brut Imperial, Bollinger Special Cuvée, or Roederer Premier, is best. True happines

> "True happiness
> Consists not in the multitude of friends,
> But in the worth and choice."
>
> —BEN JONSON, "Cynthia's Revels"

Shrimp Cocktail

The horseradish gives a wonderful bite to this cocktail sauce, but if you are sensitive to hot foods, begin with a smaller amount and sample as you go along until you hit the exact proportions that suit your tastes.

10 jumbo shrimp
1/2 cup tomato ketchup
2 teaspoons prepared horseradish (or to taste)
1 tablespoon fresh lemon juice
2 teaspoons Italian seasoning
1/2 teaspoon salt
Freshly ground black pepper to taste

Steam the shrimp in their shells for 3 to 5 minutes, or until done, then peel the shell off down to the tail and devein. Chill.

Combine the remaining ingredients, tasting for seasoning.

Serve.

TIPS

❦ To give this meal an island flair, tie the napkins with pampas grass and drink water from coconut shells.

❦ This romantic meal is nicely complemented by the music of Fred Astaire—there are several compilation albums from his 1930s movies.

Jack Tarr Potatoes

These are similar to twice-baked potatoes, except that they include grated cheese.

1 large potato
1/4 cup sour cream
1 egg, lightly beaten
1/2 cup grated sharp cheddar cheese
Salt and freshly ground black pepper to taste

Preheat the oven to 450°.

Bake the potato for 45 minutes. Remove it from the oven and let it cool a few minutes before cutting it in half lengthwise.

Carefully scoop out the potato, leaving the skin intact, and combine the potato, sour cream, egg, cheese, salt, and pepper in a small bowl.

Replace the potato mixture in the potato skins and return to the oven for 15 minutes, or until slightly browned.

Worcestershire-Grilled Lobster Tail

This is the best of the best. The marinade brings out the very best flavor of the lobster tail.

Resist buying jumbo lobster tails, because they tend to be tough. We recommend large cold-water lobster.

2 large lobster tails
4 tablespoons stick butter
1/2 teaspoon onion powder
1/4 cup fresh lemon juice
2 tablespoons Worcestershire sauce

Heat the broiler or grill.
   Melt the butter and stir in the onion powder, lemon, and Worcestershire sauce.
   To prepare the lobster tails, first make sure they're thoroughly thawed. Then, with kitchen scissors or a knife, cut a line right down to the tail fin. Pull the lobster meat out gently and set it on top of the shell (it will still be attached at the tail).
   Paint on the butter mixture.
   If you're using a grill, set the lobster down, shell side up, and cook for 10 minutes, then turn over, paint more butter mixture on, and cook another 5 to 10 minutes, or until cooked through or opaque.

If you're using a broiler, put 1/4 inch water in the broiler pan and set the lobster, shell side down, on top of the broiler rack. Paint the butter mixture on and broil for 15 minutes, reapplying the butter mixture every 5 minutes.
   Serve, using a mixture of half melted butter and half lemon as a dip.

Buttered Snow Peas

With the increasing popularity of Asian food, snow peas are becoming more and more familiar to the American. Since you eat the entire snow pea, choose the smallest and brightest-colored pods you can find. And stay away from the frozen variety . . . they are not good for much!

1 cup snow peas
2 tablespoons chopped canned water chestnuts
1 tablespoon unsalted butter
Salt and freshly ground pepper to taste

Steam the snow peas and the water chestnuts in 1/2 cup water until fork-tender, about 5 minutes. The water chestnuts will remain crispy.
   Pour into serving bowl and add butter, salt, and pepper, tossing to coat.

Poor Man's Lobster Dinner

Lemon-Pepper Grilled Shrimp
Sesame Asparagus
Herb-Roasted Tomatoes with Romano Cheese
Coconut Custard Tarts
Riesling or Chardonnay

Depending on which kind of shrimp you use, this may not exactly be a "poor man's" dinner—colossal shrimp, which some of us feel may be better than lobster, can cost up to $20 per pound, but it is certainly worth it for a special occasion. The beauty of this grilled shrimp, though, is that the marinade makes even small frozen shrimp taste delectable.

The herb-roasted tomatoes are lovely with fresh-from-the-garden summer tomatoes, and the coconut custard tarts are traditional favorites.

You may choose any dry white wine to serve with this meal, including riesling or California chardonnay.

"Champagne certainly give one werry gentlemanly ideas . . ."

—R. S. SURTEES, Mr. Jorrocks in Paris

Lemon-Pepper Grilled Shrimp

This entrée is every bit as delicious as lobster—
no small feat!

If you can find colossal shrimp or Key West
shrimp, this is a good time to go all out and use
them. Small shrimp will work as well, but since
this is a dipping dish, very much like lobster,
the larger the shrimp you can get, the better.

1 pound jumbo shrimp
1/2 cup olive oil
1/2 cup plus 3 tablespoons fresh lemon juice
2 tablespoons freshly ground black pepper
4 tablespoons butter

Combine the olive oil, 1/2 cup lemon juice, and
pepper in a bowl.

Peel the shrimp down to the tail and devein.
Marinade in oil mixture for half an hour.

Heat the grill or broiler.

Remove the shrimp from the marinade and
place on skewers.

Grill or broil for 3 to 5 minutes on each side,
or until the shrimp is cooked through. Paint
with marinade twice more during the cooking.

Meanwhile, melt the butter and combine
that with 3 tablespoons lemon juice. Use as a
dip for cooked shrimp.

Bon appétit!

Sesame Asparagus

Another Asian influence, the combination of
asparagus and sesame oil and seeds, is a
romantic culinary blending.

10 spears fresh asparagus
5 mushrooms, thinly sliced
1 teaspoon sesame oil
1 teaspoon fresh lemon juice
1/2 tablespoon sesame seeds, toasted

Fill a small sauté pan with 1/2-inch water. Bring
to a boil and add asparagus. Cover for 1 1/2
minutes or until bright green; drain and plunge
into cold water to retard the cooking process.

In a small bowl, whisk together the sesame
oil and lemon juice and stir in the sliced
mushrooms and sesame seeds.

Place the vegetables in a serving bowl and
sprinkle a few extra sesame seeds on top for
garnish.

Herb-Roasted Tomatoes with Romano Cheese

This dish alone is worth growing a few tomatoes in your backyard this summer.

2 large ripe tomatoes
2 tablespoons olive oil
1 teaspoon fresh thyme leaves
2 tablespoons grated romano cheese
Salt and freshly ground black pepper to taste

Preheat the oven to 400°.

Clean the tomatoes and cut them in half.

Heat the olive oil in a frying pan over medium-high and put the tomatoes in, cut side down. Sear them for 5 minutes (they will be almost caramelized).

Carefully move the tomatoes to a broiler pan, with the cooked side up. Drizzle with the leftover oil from the pan and top with salt, pepper, thyme, and cheese.

Bake the tomatoes, uncovered, for 30 minutes, then serve.

Coconut Custard Tarts

These tarts can be made with anything from skim milk to heavy whipping cream, which makes a lusciously creamy confection. If you're diet-conscious, half-and-half is a nice compromise.

Frozen coconut is finally available in the freezer section of most grocery stores. If you can't find that, use flake coconut (found in the baking aisle).

2 small premade pastry tart shells (you can make these by lining small tins with refrigerated pie shells, cut to fit)
1 tablespoon butter
2 tablespoons cornstarch
1 cup heavy whipping cream
1 egg, separated
1/2 teaspoon salt
1 teaspoon vanilla
1/2 cup shredded coconut
1/2 teaspoon cream of tartar

Preheat the oven to 350°.

In a small saucepan, melt the butter over medium-high heat, being careful not to brown.

Add the cornstarch and stir quickly. Immediately pour the cream in (in a steady stream), stirring constantly. Bring the mixture to a boil for 1 minute.

Lightly beat the egg yolk in a cup and stir in some of the hot liquid. Then pour the egg yolk mixture back into the saucepan, stirring constantly to keep the egg from cooking in strings. Bring the mixture back to a boil and boil for 2 minutes.

Remove the pan from the heat and stir in the salt, vanilla, and ¼ cup of coconut. Pour half into each tart shell.

Whip the egg white and cream of tartar until stiff peaks form. Spread half on each tart and top with remaining coconut.

Bake for 15 minutes, or until tops are lightly brown.

Refrigerate for at least 3 hours and serve.

TIPS

❦ Float rose petals—white for pure love, red for passion—in a crystal bowl of water and use this as a centerpiece.

❦ Natalie Cole's *Unforgettable* album is moody, romantic music for all seasons.

Cookout Chicken

Chilled Avocado Soup
Pepper-Blackened Chicken
Sautéed Spinach and Mushrooms
Anna Ruth's Southern Spoonbread
Champagne
or
Light Beer with Lemon

You might not believe it when you look at the cooking instructions for this chicken, but this makes a real summer cookout-scented (and tasting!) chicken. On the way to Ocean City, Maryland, the Lion's Club has a large charity cookout nearly every weekend in the summer, which is a favorite event for many beachgoing Marylanders. This cookout chicken is indistinguishable from that original.

Mirrasou Brut sparkling wine from Monterey, California is a creamy accompaniment to this meal, but if you prefer beer with lemon, choose a light beer, such as Corona.

"And we meet, with champagne and a chicken, at last."

—Lady Mary Wortley Montagu, "The Lover"

Chilled Avocado Soup

Avocado fans will love this cool blended soup. It's another excellent refreshment for summer and makes a nice alternative to gazpacho.

2 large ripe avocados
2 teaspoons fresh lemon juice
2 cups whole milk
Salt and freshly ground black pepper
2 teaspoons fresh chopped chives

Peel the avocados, cut them in half, and remove the pits. Chop coarsely and put them into a blender or food processor along with the lemon juice and milk and process until mixture is smooth.

Season with salt and pepper to taste.

Chill and serve garnished with chopped chives.

TIPS

❦ Issue the invitation to this dinner on a telegram. Western Union's telephone number is 1-800-325-6000.

❦ A daisy in a Coke bottle is a suitably sweet table decoration.

❦ Ella Fitzgerald's *Gershwin Songbook* or one of the Ella Fitzgerald/Louis Armstrong duet albums is fine music for this cookout.

Pepper-Blackened Chicken

You may use any or all chicken parts, but we prefer just the breasts on the bone to make this delicious dish.

2 chicken breasts on the bone
¹/₂ cup virgin olive oil
¹/₄ cup plus 2 tablespoons fresh lemon juice
3 tablespoons freshly ground black pepper
¹/₂ teaspoon salt

Combine the olive oil, lemon juice, pepper, and salt in a bowl and add the raw chicken breasts. Marinate in the refrigerator for at least an hour and preferably overnight.

Heat the grill and cook the breast, turning and basting frequently with the marinade, for 20 to 25 minutes, or until cooked through.

Sautéed Spinach and Mushrooms

Spinach is the Rodney Dangerfield of vegetables; despite a good press campaign with the Popeye guy, it still doesn't get the respect it deserves!

Spinach is among the most widely available fresh vegetables—it grows in moderately cool weather and is harvested somewhere in the world at any time. Remember that it tends to retain grit from the ground it was grown in, so it is important to wash it as many as three times. Also, remember to remove the tough stems—time-consuming, but the end result is definitely worth the trouble.

2 teaspoons peanut oil
1/2 teaspoon garlic, minced
1 pound fresh spinach
1/4 pound fresh mushrooms
Salt and freshly ground black pepper to taste

In a large sauté pan, heat oil over medium-high flame until hot. Add garlic and stir for 30 seconds. Add spinach leaves to pan and cover. Cook for 10 minutes, or until spinach cooks down.

Cut mushrooms into quarters.

Add mushrooms to spinach and sauté for 10 more minutes. Season to taste with salt and pepper.

Anna Ruth's Southern Spoonbread

The very nature of spoonbread is deeply rooted in the South, and indeed is on the Top Ten Comfort Foods List, right next to macaroni and cheese.

1/2 cup self-rising cornmeal
1/2 cup boiling water
1 1/2 tablespoons unsalted butter, melted
1/2 cup half-and-half
1 egg, well beaten
1 dash Tabasco
1/2 teaspoon butter

Preheat the oven to 375°.

In a small bowl, whisk together the boiling water, cornmeal, and melted butter. Whisk in the half-and-half and the egg, and combine until it's a thin, smooth batter. Add the Tabasco.

Grease a small glass casserole, or two ceramic ramekins, and pour in the batter.

Bake for 30 minutes.

List of Recipes